Beyond the Letter

International Library of Philosophy and Scientific Method

Editor: Ted Honderich

A Catalogue of books already published in the
International Library of Philosophy and Scientific Method
will be found at the end of this volume

Beyond the Letter

A Philosophical Inquiry into Ambiguity, Vagueness and Metaphor in Language

Israel Scheffler

Harvard University

ROUTLEDGE & KEGAN PAUL

LONDON, BOSTON AND HENLEY

First published in 1979
by Routledge & Kegan Paul Ltd
39 Store Street, London WC1E 7DD,
Broadway House, Newtown Road,
Henley-on-Thames, Oxon RG9 1EN and
9 Park Street,
Boston, Mass. 02108, USA
Set in 'Monotype' Garamond 156 by
Morrison & Gibb Ltd
Edinburgh
Printed in Great Britain by
Redwood Burn Ltd
Trowbridge & Esher

British Library Cataloguing in Publication Data

Scheffler, Israel

Beyond the letter. – (International library
of philosophy and scientific method).
1. Languages – Philosophy 2. Ambiguity
3. Metaphor
I. Title II. Series
401   P106   79-40095

ISBN 0 7100 0315 3

For Rosalind

CONTENTS

Preface

Introduction   I
1   *Idealization and Deviation*   I
2   *Varieties of Understanding*   2
3   *Theoretical Accounts and Their Difficulties*   7
4   *Inscriptionalistic Assumptions*   8

I   Ambiguity   11
1   *Introduction to the Problem*   11
2   *Inscriptions and Extensions: Elementary Ambiguity*   12
3   *E-ambiguity, Generality, Vagueness*   14
4   *Ambiguity of Occurrence: I-ambiguity*   15
5   *Ambiguity of Occurrence: M-ambiguity*   17
6   *A New Problem: Green Centaurs*   20
7   *Difference in Meaning*   22
8   *Constituent Ambiguity*   27
9   *Compound Ambiguity*   29
10   *Mention-selection*   31

II   Vagueness   37
1   *Vagueness and I-ambiguity*   37
2   *Vagueness, Generality, Precision*   40
3   *Vagueness and Molecular Compounds*   43
4   *Vagueness, Atomic Compounds and Mention-selection*   45

5   Relativity and the Universality of Vagueness   49
6   The Possibility of Vagueness   50
7   Open texture, Compounds and Mention-selection   51
8   Open texture and Analyticity   53
9   Open texture and Relative Terms   57
10 Open texture and Classification   60
11 Vagueness and Logic   65
12 Vagueness, Meaning and Fact   72

III Metaphor   79
1   Metaphor, Mention-selection and E-ambiguity   79
2   Intuitionistic Approach to Metaphor   82
3   Emotivism and Metaphor   87
4   Formulaic Approach to Metaphor   92
5   Intensional Approach to Metaphor   97
6   Evaluation of Intensionalism   100
7   Interactionism and Metaphor   107
8   Evaluation of Interactionism   110
9   Contextualism and Metaphor   118
10 Evaluation of Contextualism   124
11 Metaphor and Exploration   128

Notes   131
Index   144

ACKNOWLEDGMENTS

The author and publishers wish to thank the following for permission to reproduce copyright material:

For extracts from *Languages of Art* permission granted by Nelson Goodman, Second Edition, 1976, Hackett Publishing Company, Inc., PO Box 55576, Indianapolis, Indiana 46205 for USA and Canada, and Harvester Ltd, Sussex.

Prentice-Hall, Inc. for extracts from *Philosophy of Logic*, 1970, by W. V. Quine, and *Philosophy of Language*, 1964, by William P. Alston.

The Bobbs-Merrill Company, Inc. for extracts from *Logic & Art: Essays in Honor of Nelson Goodman*, 1972, ed. Richard Rudner and Israel Scheffler.

For an extract from *Aesthetics* by Monroe C. Beardsley, © 1958 by Harcourt Brace Jovanovich, Inc. and reprinted with their permission.

The Aristotelian Society and Professor Max Black for extracts from 'Metaphor' by Max Black, published in the *Proceedings of the Aristotelian Society*, vol. 55 (new series), 1954.

Professor Max Black and Professor Carl G. Hempel and The Williams & Wilkins Co. for extracts from 'Vagueness: An Exercise in Logical Analysis', by Max Black, published in *Philosophy of Science*, vol. 4 (1937), and 'Vagueness and Logic' by Carl G. Hempel published in *Philosophy of Science*, vol. 6 (1939), © The Williams & Wilkins Co., Baltimore.

PREFACE

Ambiguity, vagueness, and metaphor are pervasive features of language, deserving of analytical study in their own right. Yet they have frequently been treated as mere deviations from the semantic ideal or as obstacles to be avoided in constructing systems. In this book, I attempt a consecutive philosophical treatment of these features and their relations to one another, studying related problems along the way.

My general interest in these topics goes back almost to the time of my dissertation work on indirect discourse. Like that work and like several of my publications since, the present study is nominalistic in its philosophical orientation, taking only inscriptions as its linguistic elements and forswearing the Platonism of traditional semantics. This strategy helps, I believe, to protect against philosophical question-begging: it may also help bring to light points of general interest. If such there be here, they can readily be accommodated by other orientations than the inscriptional.

Topics are presented in what has seemed to me a natural order. For example, the analysis of ambiguity in Part I characterizes metaphor as a special case, which is then treated in Part III; the significance of compounds, emphasized in Part I, is elaborated further in Part II; and the idea of mention-selection, first introduced in the discussion of ambiguity, figures in both later Parts. The order in which topics may be read is, however, not firmly fixed; some readers will find it desirable to start with the treatment of metaphor in Part III, requiring only occasional flashbacks for special points, and leaving for later the more technical discussions of the earlier Parts.

The ideas presented here have been discussed in courses and seminars of mine since 1967. In the Fall of that year, Sylvain Bromberger and I offered a joint seminar in philosophy of language, which touched on certain of the issues to be treated. Preliminary versions of some sections of Parts I and II formed the substance of lectures to philosophy colloquia at the Hebrew University, the Rockefeller University, the University of Miami, The University of Notre Dame, and Brown University. Part I, in an earlier version and lacking Section 5, appeared in *Logic and Art: Essays in Honor of Nelson Goodman* (1972), edited by Richard Rudner and myself; I am grateful to the publisher, the Bobbs-Merrill Company, for permission to reprint.

As will be evident to any philosophically informed reader, I am deeply indebted to Nelson Goodman in the studies reported here. My thinking on related matters has been strongly influenced as well by W.V. Quine. Robert Schwartz and Margaret Atherton met periodically with me during 1969–70 for discussion of my ideas on ambiguity; I am grateful to them for illuminating comments and criticism. I am also grateful to Dr Avishai Margalit, with whom I discussed various issues in the philosophy of language during 1974–5. And I owe special thanks to Professor Robert Schwartz, Professor Gilbert H. Harman and Professor Vernon A. Howard, who all read an earlier version of the present text and made important comments and suggestions, of which I have tried to take account. I trust that no one will suppose any of those I have mentioned to be responsible for the shortcomings of my treatment and formulations.

Some of the preliminary work for this book was begun during a sabbatical leave in 1958–9 and continued during another in 1972–3; for these leaves I am grateful to Harvard University. I wish to express my thanks to the John Simon Guggenheim Memorial Foundation, which supported my work during both these periods. In 1972–3, I was a Fellow of the Center for Advanced Study in the Behavioral Sciences. I am grateful for the support and hospitality of the Center and the opportunity for exchange of ideas with a variety of scholars, of whom I must mention, in particular, Professors Steven Marcus, Herbert Weiner, M.D., and Joseph Weizenbaum. I thank the William F.

Milton Fund of Harvard University for support that facilitated the research in its final stages and the preparation of the manuscript.

To Laurie Scheffler I am indebted for help with citations and preliminary work on the index. For library research and for preparation of the index I am grateful to Jean Hampton, who also provided me with valuable substantive comments. I thank Shirley Foster, who prepared the complete final typescript and assisted with the proofs.

My indebtedness to my wife, to whom this book is dedicated, is beyond measure.

Israel Scheffler

Newton, Massachusetts

INTRODUCTION

I IDEALIZATION AND DEVIATION

Philosophical and other studies have often been guided by an ideal conception of language as utterly precise, determinate, purely literal and perfectly univocal. Theorists have, of course, recognized that actual languages fall far short of such an ideal conception. They have, however, hoped eventually to illumine the actual features and operations of language by initial consideration of simplified structures. Such idealization is certainly a legitimate strategy of inquiry, but its explanatory success in any given case depends on clear understanding of the simplified structure itself, as well as the availability of principled judgments as to actual deviations from it.[1] On both counts, the idealization of language mentioned above has been far from satisfactory: It has not been evident how exactly to interpret such concepts as precision, determinacy, univocality, and literalness, nor have we been offered an adequate understanding of how expressions may fall short of their perfect embodiment.

The present work is addressed to this situation. In particular, it attempts a direct study of lapses or deviations from the prevalent semantic ideal, its aim being to further theoretical comprehension of such "deviational" phenomena as ambiguity, vagueness, metaphor, and related aspects of language. The characterization of such features as 'deviational' is, however, relative to an ideal conception that can itself not be taken for granted. This characterization must emphatically not be taken to imply that these features are isolated, fragmentary or merely privative. On the contrary, they are pervasive, important, and deserving of systematic study in their own right. Beyond the ideal code, the bare letter of language, they contribute its typical shape and force, its normal appearance and flow. Any advance in our understanding of these features will, moreover, not only enrich our appreciation of language, but also help to clarify the status of attempted idealizations.

To say that ambiguity, vagueness, and metaphor are, at present, not adequately understood requires qualification, however. In providing such qualification, the discussion to follow will serve to define the scope of the present study and to make explicit its major philosophical presuppositions.

2   VARIETIES OF UNDERSTANDING

It might be denied, first of all, that the features that concern us are insufficiently understood, for people do generally claim to recognize instances of ambiguous or vague or metaphorical expressions in practice. Such practical skill is, however, perfectly compatible with a lack of theoretical comprehension, that is, an inability to offer a general account of the skill, or a specification of the criteria ingredient to its exercise. We all learn to identify expressions, with more or less confidence, as ambiguous or vague or metaphorical. But this is far from saying that we all have a general theory or definition or explication of ambiguity or vagueness or metaphor. To provide a general or theoretical account resting upon instances of practice is a characteristically philosophical task, and it is just such a task that we undertake with respect to the features of language in question.

It might, nevertheless, be insisted that these features not only acquire a degree of identifiability in practice, but also fall within the province of several intellectual specialties. Literary critics and analysts have, for example, shown a profound interest in the phenomena in question and made valuable contributions to their appreciation. They have, understandably enough, however, given their attention mainly to the interpretation of particular instances occurring in literary works. Such interpretation of instances provides important material for philosophical generalization, but it does not, any more than the common recognition of instances, constitute a general theory or philosophical account. Indeed, it must itself employ general conceptions, presupposed as suitable for analytical purposes. Where such conceptions are held to be intuitively clear, their mere employment as interpretive instruments certainly does not constitute explication. Where proffered explications are borrowed from the common stock of notions, they typically fail of sufficient rigor. Where, finally, they are newly constructed for the critical tasks at hand, they are frequently limited in scope or otherwise philosophically inadequate, despite their usefulness in application.[2]

Psychologists, psychoanalytically oriented thinkers, and philosophers of culture have also concerned themselves with the features of language that we have been discussing, and they have provided a rich context for the study of these features. They have sought to employ them as clues to the nature of thought processes, and have also suggested genetic interpretations of ambiguity and of metaphor.[3] Whereas the literary analysts tend to focus on instances thought to *exemplify* the features in question, the theorists now under consideration strive to *relate* these features to other properties, pertaining either to mental life or to social circumstances. Such efforts, however, also presuppose the availability of suitable concepts applicable to the linguistic features involved. To assume these concepts intuitively clear at the outset provides no theory at all, whereas to borrow common interpretations or develop new constructions for local genetic or psychological applications is not likely to yield philosophical satisfaction.

Lexicographers, it may be said, are certainly involved in a consideration of the linguistic features in question in the process of writing entries. But the lexicographer's judgments – of ambiguity, for example – themselves require theoretical analysis and systematic description. His judgments do not differ, except in experience and range, from those of the common language user with the normal practical ability to identify instances of the features we have been discussing. What is wanted is an analysis of the bases of his judgments. Certainly the dictionary that issues from his efforts is no such analysis; it is rather an application than an explication of his semantical notions.[4]

Nor does it help matters to say that he is not relying on his own

3

semantical conceptions but is rather attempting to reflect or predict those of his informants. For if he takes certain usages of these informants as grounds for ascribing to their expressions a certain ambiguity, say, which he intends his dictionary to report, he continues to employ a notion of ambiguity of his own in characterizing his informants' usage. On the other hand, if, disclaiming such independent characterization, he asks his informants directly to say which expressions are ambiguous and intends his dictionary entries simply to reflect *their* responses, he is indeed no longer characterizing expressions as 'ambiguous' but only as 'commonly labeled "ambiguous" '. The question remains, however, as to the bases of the informant's original labeling: *he* has not in turn applied the notion 'commonly labeled "ambiguous" ', but has rather called certain expressions 'ambiguous' directly. What general account can be given of the underlying ground of these judgments?[5]

The lexicographer may alternatively, perhaps, be understood as *defining* a notion of ambiguity of his own by reference to the unanalyzed judgments of informants: he may be interpreted as saying that an expression is ambiguous if and only if it is called 'ambiguous' by his informants. Such a proposal may be conceded to supply a clear and applicable stipulation. It cannot, however, be assumed to define the notion employed either by the informants in question or by the lexicographer himself in everyday contexts, where he serves as his own informant. Nor is there any antecedent reason to suppose that the stipulation in question provides a useful theoretical replacement for the everyday notion, incorporating, as it does, the informants' unanalyzed understandings of the very term it would replace. There is no reason to assume that the incorporation of such understandings, statistically idealized, offers the promise of theoretical insight into the linguistic features addressed. What is wanted is independent theoretical analysis of semantical concepts, not descriptions embodying popular construals of these concepts. It is one thing to offer an independent theoretical definition of 'congruent' or 'neurotic' or 'subjunctive' and quite another to define these terms as referring, respectively, to whatever is *called* 'congruent' or 'neurotic' or 'subjunctive' by chosen informants.[6]

Logicians and philosophers have also taken considerable interest in the linguistic features we have been discussing. On the whole, however, their attitude toward these features has been primarily a practical one. They are quick to note them polemically in assaying the arguments of others, resting their judgments not on theory but on intuition. Correlatively, they are alive to these features as defects to be eliminated from their own serious constructions, often in defense against the polemics of others. Occasionally, they have taken as their aim the devising of a language with ideal suitability for scientific purposes, maximally clear and regimented by stated rules. Short of *devising* such a language, they have at times striven at least to *characterize* a language with ideal scientific attributes. Such efforts at characterization have, however, typically failed to analyze the features in question, rather presupposing their intuitive identifiability.

Treating the use of logical formalisms in evaluating implications in ordinary discourses, logicians have indeed recognized the preliminary task of processing ordinary statements and replacing them by fitting symbolic formulations. 'The task of thus suitably paraphrasing a statement and isolating the relevant structure is just as essential to the application of logic as is the test or proof of implication for which that preliminary task prepares the way,' writes W.V. Quine. Noting the availability of certain partial methods of paraphrase, he remarks, however, that in the matter of ascertaining the intended grouping of constituent clauses, we must 'in the main . . . rely on our good sense of everyday idiom for a sympathetic understanding of the statement and then re-think the whole in logical symbols.'[7]

Even in the more limited matter of avoiding equivocation in the paraphrase of component clauses, the logician's concern is to eliminate only such equivocations as result from the varying effects of immediate contexts on a given expression, yielding differing interpretations within the scope of the argument in question. He is not interested in equivocations that do not affect the interior of the argument, nor in those that do not touch the assignments of truth-values or extensions to constituent expressions. In general, his aim is to achieve reliable methods of judging the validity of inference – to develop formalisms that will carry truths into truths when applied to the suitably processed materials of ordinary discourse. His treatment of *suitable processing* is an adjunct to his theoretical work with particular formalisms and concerns only the practical matter of their application. It is thus limited in function and indeed stops far short of a general analysis of those features of ordinary language which we have been discussing.

The standpoint of philosophers and logicians has grown out of a preoccupation with the improvement of language for scientific description and systematization. From this standpoint, they have tended to think of vaguenesses, ambiguities, and metaphors mainly as obstacles to be overcome, as deviations from the ideal. They have, accordingly, often taken the main philosophical problem presented by such phenomena to be the devising of methods for overcoming them wholly or approximately in the construction of scientific and philosophical languages. Though understandable, this attitude is, however, surely too restrictive. For our theoretical languages are also to be employed in the description of language as a natural phenomenon – embodying, among other things, those very features we may have striven to expunge from its description. Thus the task of providing a theoretical analysis of such features presents itself. To admit them as objects of our descriptive efforts does not commit us to incorporating them into our descriptive language. Conversely, to bar them, as far as possible, from our descriptive apparatus in no way commits us to denying their existence in actual instances of language use. It is possible, in short, to strive for a clear, literal and precise account of such phenomena as vagueness, ambiguity, and metaphor. And such a goal defines a theoretical task of analysis and description that reaches far beyond the practical attitude we have been discussing.

Turning from the object domain of physical phenomena to that of natural language, philosophers have often approached the latter with attitudes more appropriate to management of the theoretical languages with which they had been concerned. Accordingly, they have tended to minimize devices of language prevalent in everyday contexts and intensified in literary and poetic discourses. Noting that the ambiguity of a term may not be resolved by its containing sentence, W.V. Quine remarks, 'Then either it is resolved by broader circumstances of utterance . . . , or else communication fails and a paraphrase is in order.'[8] Here the notion of communication itself is so construed as to exclude everyday cases of interpretive indecision and "multiple meaning" as well as the studied ambiguities of the poet.

Ambiguity may indeed represent a failure in languages constructed for theoretical use; in the poet's hands, it is generally not a failure but an instrument of expression. The concept of communication must be kept wide enough to embrace the devices of poet as well as common speaker. The constraints of theory are not opposed to the recognition of poetry.

3   THEORETICAL ACCOUNTS AND THEIR DIFFICULTIES

What has been said so far does not imply that there have been *no* attempts to provide a theoretical account of the linguistic features that concern us. I think it fair to say, however, that such philosophical accounts as have been offered are typically partial and that none has been generally persuasive. On the contrary, competing interpretations are normally available, with differences that have been, for the most part, unresolved.

Available accounts are, moreover, vulnerable to several forms of deficiency which may be summarized as follows: First, the appeal to dictionary-related concepts in explanation is inadequate, as we have argued above. Secondly, as earlier remarked, certain forms of reliance on informants constitute evasions of the question; consider, for example, the definition recently offered by two theorists: 'The meanings of a word . . . to a particular person may be characterized by describing the responses he makes . . . when asked for its "meaning".'[9] Thirdly, the assimilation of natural languages to artificial languages with explicit rules and fixed interpretations is groundless and question-begging. Fourthly, there is a persistent temptation to explain the obscure by appeal to the no less obscure: Consider, for example, the explanation of ambiguity as the possession of more than one meaning; surely the latter property is no less problematic than the former and is therefore worthless in explanation.

It must, finally, be noted that the traditional semantic apparatus has undergone severe criticism over the past few decades. The details of this criticism make a long story which cannot be reviewed here.[10] Suffice it to say that the notions criticized include those of synonymy and analyticity, of intensional entities such as concepts, properties, attributes, meanings, propositions, facts and states-of-affairs, of modalities, essences, and truths expressible by counterfactual constructions. They include, moreover, even the notion of sets, which is, if anything, clearer than the items previously listed.[11]

The critique mentioned has, of course, not been accepted by everyone. Moreover, even those who, like myself, have accepted some or all of it have not as yet carried through the reinterpretation of semantics indicated. Semantics remains, in various regions of application, abstract, intensional, and necessitarian or essentialistic, as well as dependent upon the myth of the official dictionary or official rule-book. From the point of view of the critics, this situation is theoretically intolerable: We need to free our understanding of language from dependence upon notions that are obscure, or else admit that such understanding, if it is not itself illusory, constitutes an as yet unsolved problem.

4 INSCRIPTIONALISTIC ASSUMPTIONS

I propose, then, to avoid reliance upon traditional notions of analyticity and synonymy, modal and counterfactual constructions, and purportedly essential features of objects or elements. I make no assumption of intensional entities, that is to say, Platonic objects such as concepts, attributes, properties, propositions, facts, states-of-affairs or, in particular, meanings. I do not presuppose the availability of uniquely decisive rule-books or dictionaries governing the interpretation of problematic expressions. Finally, I surrender theoretical dependence upon sets, classes, sequences, or other abstract objects, though they are not intensional: the point, in particular, is to avoid ultimate appeal to types as distinct from tokens, that is, utterances and inscriptions. Applied to semantical topics, the nominalistic attitude here outlined may be labeled *inscriptionalism*. The label implies no theoretical contrast with nominalism; it simply calls attention to the favored status of tokens, and the exclusion of types, classes, meanings, forms, and attributes from our semantic apparatus.

The significance of such exclusion may be seen by reference to the semantic scheme inherited from the past and widespread in contemporary use. This scheme recognizes not merely the particular 'dog'-utterances and 'dog'-inscriptions that historically occur, but also an additional object identified with the word 'dog',

8

construed as an abstract entity of some sort – a form, or class, or sequence of sound or letter tokens. It recognizes not merely the individual dogs denoted by the word, but the denotation of the word – an abstract entity identified with the class of dogs denoted. The denotation is, further, construed to be determined by the word's meaning, identified or associated with the attribute of being a dog, itself exemplified by members of the denotation. Concepts, propositions, facts, and states-of-affairs may be introduced additionally, and related in diverse ways to the foregoing objects. The individuation of entities in this scheme, finally, rests at various points on presumed synonymies, analyticities, modal judgments, essences, counterfactual assertions, or intuitive descriptions of the supposed entities in question.

Inscriptionalism, by contrast, takes for granted only the individual tokens and the individual things that may be denoted. Neither abstract entities associated with tokens nor those associated with denoted things, nor intensional intermediaries between tokens and things are, in short, to be employed as unanalyzed tools of semantic interpretation. The underlying nominalistic idea is an old one but it has recently reappeared and been applied to a variety of problem areas.[12]

Since tokens and denoted things are assumed by any semantic scheme, inscriptionalism does not *add to* the entities commonly recognized; its interpretations are therefore ontologically acceptable to non-inscriptionalists, although the converse does not hold. Readers who do not share the inscriptionalistic assumptions of the present inquiry may therefore still find interest in its interpretations. They need not take its exclusions in any absolute sense, but only understand them hypothetically, as defining the methodological constraints of the study. They may, moreover, be assured that notions excluded by these constraints may be reintroduced at will by anyone who does not find them obscure.

The plan of the present inquiry is, then, to consider in order the subjects of ambiguity, vagueness, and metaphor, seeking in each case interpretations that will be materially adequate and will, moreover, satisfy inscriptionalistic constraints. We address ourselves first to the topic of ambiguity.

I

AMBIGUITY

What is ambiguity? Under what conditions is a word ambiguous? We all claim a certain practical facility in spotting ambiguities, but the theory of the matter is in a sorry state. Logicians and philosophers typically concern themselves with ambiguity either as a defect in the arguments of others or as a hazard from which their own serious discourse is to be protected. Literary critics, alive to the rhetorical values of ambiguous expression, are not equally sensitive to the philosophical demands for clarity and system. General analytical questions thus remain for the most part unexplored, while commonly repeated explanations suffer from various grave difficulties.

A word is, for example, said to be ambiguous if it has different meanings or senses, or if it stands for different ideas. But ghostly entities such as meanings, senses, or ideas provide no more than the ghost of an explanation unless, as seems unlikely, they can be clearly construed as countable things whose relations to one another and to words are independently determinable. At best, such entities may be regarded as hypostatizations of the content of sets of synonymous expressions, the specification resting on the critically obscure notion of synonymy.

In more concrete vein, a word may be said to be ambiguous in having different dictionary readings, that is, in being correlated with different actual expressions in the dictionary. But which dictionary is to be chosen and how has it been composed? Are the principles by which its readings have been assigned clearly formulable; are they unique; can we be confident that they themselves make no appeal to the lexicographer's unanalyzed judgments of ambiguity?

We must, moreover, ask in what the relevant difference of readings consists. The readings in question are presumably to be not merely different but non-synonymous; the proposed criterion of ambiguity thus presupposes, without providing an account of, the troublesome notion of synonymy. Alternatively, it may be suggested that we consider not different actual expressions, but different abstract readings, a reading to be construed now as an entity correlated with a set of synonymous expressions; here the individuation of readings clearly hinges on synonymy, and their postulation carries us back to meanings or senses once more.

Furthermore, the criterion at best falls short of providing a sufficient condition, since non-synonymous readings, however construed, may signify generality rather than ambiguity. For the word 'caravan', for instance, we find the following two readings:[2]

(i) A group of travelers journeying together through desert or hostile regions.
(ii) A group of vehicles traveling together in a file.

Is it clear that these two readings signify the ambiguity of 'caravan' rather than mark out two regions of its general, and unambiguous, application?

Finally, are the expressions representing the readings themselves assumed to be purified of ambiguity? Unless they are, we cannot take the lack of non-synonymous readings for a given word to betoken its freedom from ambiguity. On the other hand, to require these expressions themselves to be unambiguous renders the criterion, as a whole, circular.

2   INSCRIPTIONS AND EXTENSIONS: ELEMENTARY
AMBIGUITY

The proposals just considered have this in common: Between words and denoted things they interpose additional entities as the root of ambiguity – meanings or senses or ideas or readings – entities whose individuation or explanatory role is obscure, involving, at the very least, appeal to the controverted notion of synonymy. Can any progress be made by wiping the slate clean, renouncing such interposition altogether and restricting ourselves to words and ordinary things? Will an inscriptional approach, moreover, considering word-tokens only and surrendering the notion of associated abstract types, enable us to advance the analysis of ambiguity?

An elementary inscriptional account may be sketched, as follows: We treat written tokens only and, among these, attend only to predicate tokens. These, however, are given to us embedded in naturally occurring contexts which enable us, generally, to judge certain of their denotative relations. Then, for any two predicate tokens x and y, we ask:

(i) Are x and y spelled exactly alike, i.e. are they replicas of one another?

(ii) Are x and y extensionally divergent, i.e. does either one denote something not denoted by the other?

Given tokens x and y for which the answers to the above two questions are both positive, we now say they are ambiguous with respect to one another. Further, given simply x, we hold it ambiguous if there is some token y with respect to which it is ambiguous. To mark these *elementary* notions of ambiguity from other varieties to be introduced, we may say that x and y are E-ambiguous with respect to one another when they stand in the relation specified, and that x is E-ambiguous (categorically) if E-ambiguous with respect to some y.

(To judge extensional divergence or equivalence, note that it is not required to determine the elements in fact denoted by x and y. Interpreting any of a variety of contextual cues, we may reasonably gauge the divergence or equivalence of x and y without determining particular things denoted by either.)

This account needs, however, to be limited to a particular discourse D to become effective for, as it stands, it characterizes x as E-ambiguous if it has an extensionally divergent replica y in some other language, or remote context. The condition it sets is far too weak and, hence, satisfied by vastly more predicate tokens than are ordinarily deemed ambiguous. That x fulfils this condition is compatible with its being perfectly unambiguous within the space of some restricted discourse of interest. We thus amplify the account by adding that x is E-ambiguous relative to discourse D if, and only if, x belongs to D and is E-ambiguous with respect to some y belonging to D. Clearly, there will now be suitably many unambiguous tokens relative to limited discourses under consideration.

The proposal just sketched is circumscribed. It restricts itself to predicate tokens, and does not deal with other sorts of word-tokens nor with word-sequences of sentence length or more. It gives no account of syntactic ambiguities, but treats only ambiguity of a semantic sort. Yet it covers an undeniably important variety, of the same sort with which we have, in fact, been concerned from the beginning, and earlier accounts of which we found wanting in our previous discussion.

3 E-AMBIGUITY, GENERALITY, VAGUENESS

The idea of the above proposal is set forth by Goodman from the point of view of a primary interest in indicator terms:[3]

> Roughly speaking, a word is an *indicator* if . . . it names something not named by some replica of the word. This is admittedly broad, including ambiguous terms as well as what might be regarded as indicators-proper, such as pronouns; but delimitation of the narrower class of indicators-proper is a ticklish business and is not needed for our present purposes.

The inclusive category is, from the point of view of our present concerns, that of *ambiguity*, with indicators forming one subgroup of ambiguous terms, roughly distinguishable by the fact that extensional variation across indicator-replicas is related, in a relatively systematic manner, to some contextual feature of these replicas. Thus, an 'I' normally refers to its own producer and a 'now' to a suitable time period within which its own production lies. Another subgroup is constituted by metaphorical terms, a metaphorical predicate within D roughly characterizable as having therein some extensionally divergent replica offering, in some manner, a clue to its own application.

Elementary ambiguity, as above interpreted, is distinguishable from generality in that a token E-ambiguous within D must diverge extensionally from some replica therein. If no such divergence exists, the fact that a token applies to many things signifies only that it is general, no matter how dissimilar these things may be, by whatever criteria of similarity may be chosen. That a 'table' denotes big as well as little tables argues not its ambiguity but only its breadth of applicability. Though perhaps difficult to apply in certain instances, the distinction will nevertheless be effective in many others. In a 'This book contains a table of contents on page 4', the constituent 'table' token diverges extensionally from its replica in 'A table is an essential article of furniture'. Philosophical disputes as to whether some critical term, e.g. 'exists', *should* be construed as ambiguous, or merely general, may hinge on far-reaching theoretical considerations.[4] The problem of settling the construction of a term for special theoretical purposes is different, however, from that of interpreting given expressions within ordinary discourses. At any rate, the purport of even the philosophical issue may be clarified by the distinction.

Elementary ambiguity will also be distinguishable from vagueness, where the latter is taken to involve a certain indeterminacy or ambivalence in deciding the applicability of a term to an object. For x, vague relative to some object o, may yet be E-unambiguous relative to D, having either no replicas at all within D or only such as are co-extensive and (perhaps even) alike indeterminate respecting o. Conversely, x and y may be ambiguous with respect to one another, neither displaying vagueness relative to any o within our domain of consideration. Indicators provide the most striking, if not the only, examples, each of several 'I' tokens within a given D being, we may imagine, clearly decidable in its denotation, which yet varies from that of each other replica within D.

4 AMBIGUITY OF OCCURRENCE: I-AMBIGUITY

Elementary ambiguity, therefore, does not altogether accord with usual understandings. It consists in extensional variation among replicas, each of which may, however, be perfectly definite in the way we apply it. Reverting to the language of types, we may say it is a feature of variability of the type rather than a species of variability characterizing the single occurrence;

moreover, the type variability may occasion no problem of decision. On the other hand, we often convey, in calling an expression 'ambiguous', that there is some difficulty attaching to its interpretation *in a given occurrence*, some *indecision affecting the single token*. Such a point has been often noted. Hospers, for example, writes, 'Sometimes, in fact, the very word "ambiguity" is restricted so as to mean only *misleading* ambiguity . . .'.[5] Richman distinguishes 'semantical ambiguity', as the possession of more than one meaning by an expression, from 'psychological ambiguity', as the occurrence of a semantically ambiguous expression in a context in which the intended interpretation is unclear.[6] Quine remarks that 'ambiguity is supposed to consist in indecisiveness between meanings.'[7] Having here renounced the notion of meanings, can we account for indecision respecting the individual token, a feature not implied by elementary ambiguity in itself?

To assimilate such indecision to mere vagueness would miss the crucial point that, as Richman puts it, 'psychological ambiguity involves semantical ambiguity'[8]; the indecision affecting the given token must be related to the fact that its type is ambiguous. But we have already mirrored type variability inscriptionalistically in the notion of elementary ambiguity, so our problem is to relate the indecision now in question to elementary ambiguity. Suppose then replicas z, y, and x, with z and y decidably divergent in extension, hence E-ambiguous with respect to one another. Assume x embedded in a context C that does not rule out its being extensionally equivalent either to z or to y: To interpret x as extensionally equivalent to z or to y will make maximally good sense of C and, let us imagine, better sense than the assignment to x of a wholly different extension. Either interpretation will enable us to understand what attribution is accomplished in C by the presence of x. Yet we cannot find sufficient reason to choose between them; the alternative interpretations are equally reasonable. Here is an inscriptional example, readily generalizable, of what Quine calls 'indecisiveness between meanings', the indecisiveness concerning alignment of x with one or another divergent replica, each providing in itself the clue to a plausible interpretation.[9] Where x is characterized by such indecision, we shall describe it as I-ambiguous (relative to context C).

5   AMBIGUITY OF OCCURRENCE: *M*-AMBIGUITY

Neither *E*-ambiguity nor *I*-ambiguity is adequate to another sort of ambiguity attaching to the single token – involving a species of so-called multiple meaning. Here, as with *I*-ambiguity, we are concerned not with mere type variability but with a kind of interpretive variability in the occurrence. Whereas, however, the difficulty in interpreting an *I*-ambiguous token arises from the need to choose between rival extensions, the difficulty now to be discussed lies rather in the need not to choose between such rival extensions, but to hold on to them simultaneously.

The *I*-ambiguous token has one extension but too meager a context to allow us a decision as to which it is. (As Richman describes the situation, '*the* intended interpretation is not clear.')[10] By contrast, the *M*-ambiguous token (i.e. the token with multiple meaning) appears to have simultaneously different extensions. It is moreover not the case, as Quine supposes, that either the ambiguity 'is resolved by broader circumstances of utterance . . . , or else communication fails and a paraphrase is in order.'[11] Lack of resolution as between rival extensions signals communicative failure only if the intended interpretation is unique. If, however, the effort is precisely to make *multiple* statements by means of a single token, the inability to discard any of these statements indicates success. The problem is to say how a single token can make different statements, how a predicate token can simultaneously support different extensions, without contradiction.

Since the problem concerns *simultaneous* differences, it cannot be resolved by the time-slicing of an enduring physical object, taking each slice as a different token with at most a single extension. And, it should be emphasized, the problem that concerns us has to do not just with diverse meaning-attributions but specifically with those that conflict. A given token may indeed express or exemplify one thing while at the same time denoting another, but it cannot both denote and at the same time fail to denote the same thing.

The *M*-ambiguous token, then, threatens us with inconsistency. For if *M*-ambiguous *x* has two different extensions, there is an object *o* that belongs to one but not the other, and therefore is both denoted and not denoted by *x*. Yet, *M*-ambiguity is a widespread occurrence. Puns provide the clearest illustration, although the phenomenon is much more general and is basic in poetry. Quine's sample sentence,[12]

Our mothers bore us,

which he treats as exemplifying I-ambiguity, is more naturally taken as a case of M-ambiguity, for the word 'bore' is a pun, denoting both bores and bearers (ignoring tense, for simplicity's sake). The pun requires *both* references; it is not a matter of deciding upon the *unique* intended reference. Yet both references cannot, without contradiction, be attributed to the same term.

Nor can we readily relativize denotation to languages or systems, so as to allow the same token to have one extension in a given language, for example, and another in a different language. In the first place, tokens, unlike types, do not individually recur in different linguistic or systematic contexts, and it is not clear that such contexts overlap suitably, i.e. that different languages can be interpreted appropriately as laying claim to the same M-ambiguous inscriptions. Secondly, it is in general not evident how languages or systems are to be individuated. In Quine's words, 'What is a language? What degree of fixity is supposed? When do we have one language and not two?'[13] Finally, it is difficult to interpret the relevant notion of a language inscriptionalistically, and without reliance upon the myth of official dictionaries or rule-books.

Like the I-ambiguous token, the M-ambiguous token x has replicas z and y decidably divergent in extension. Presented with x in context, and starting with the presumption that it has a unique extension, we find it impossible to decide whether to align it uniquely with z or y. The context allows either decision, and the resultant irresolution so far mirrors the case of I-ambiguity. However, unlike the latter case, irresolution here sparks the (typically sudden) realization that neither plan makes maximally good sense of the relevant context – that in fact two statements are being made at once through the medium of x, thus rebutting the presumption that it has a unique extension. But if it cannot be assigned a single extension, neither can it be assigned more than one, as we have seen.

The source of the problem may be thought to be an oversupply of *extensions*: we have more putative extensions than we have tokens to carry them: one such extension apiece for z and y, and two for x. However, the latter two are identical with the first two, respectively; we thus have actually only two extensions for the three tokens in question. But the putative double extension of x gives rise (in the simplest case) to two statements attached to the single sentential context of x, neither of which is normally identifiable with the statement attached to the context of z or of y. Thus we have rather an oversupply of *statements* relative to available *sentence tokens*. What we need is a sentence token for each putative statement; in particular, we require two sentence tokens to bear the two statements conveyed by the single sentential context of x. Is there a way of splitting the latter context into two appropriate tokens?

A sentence token is a whole made up of word tokens with appropriate mutual orientations and spacing, arranged grammatically in normal linear order. An otherwise suitable whole that has all but one word inscription in Boston and the remaining word inscription in Buffalo is not indeed a sentence token. If the place of the missing inscription is marked by a word-space, however, then the whole composed of the Boston token, with its space, and the Buffalo word token is a clearly *potential* sentence. For it is only the wrong relative location of the Boston and Buffalo tokens that prevents actual sentencehood, the right location for the missing word being decisively indicated by the word-space. Though potential *as a sentence*, this scattered sentential whole is an actual individual, moreover, consisting wholly of tokens.[14]

The notion of a scattered whole comprising a potential sentence now suggests a way of "splitting" the sentential context of x. For corresponding to the latter context, we have in fact two relevant potential sentences, one consisting of x's sentential frame plus z, and the other consisting of the same frame plus y (z and y being replicas of x with decidably divergent extensions). These two potential sentences may now be associated, respectively, with the two statements conveyed by the single sentential context of x.

To get a clearer idea of this suggestion, let us supply names for the three sentential frames in question, that of x, that of z, and that of y: Call x's frame 'K', z's frame 'L', and y's frame 'N'. What we have referred to as the sentential context of x is, then, composed of $x+K$; analogously, the sentential context of z is

$z+L$, and that of y is $y+N$. While x, z, and y are replicas, we assume that (as in the typical case) K is not a replica of L or of N, nor is L a replica of N. Moreover, we suppose also (as in the typical case) that neither of the putative statements conveyed by $x+K$ is identical with the statement made by $z+L$ or with that made by $y+N$. Now one of the putative statements of $x+K$ is interpretable as what *would be* conveyed by it were x extensionally equivalent to z; the other statement of $x+K$ is interpretable as what *would be* conveyed by it if x were coextensive with y. Finally, we remove the subjunctive locutions altogether, replacing them, respectively, with references to the concrete potential sentences $z+K$ and $y+K$ (or, equivalently, $z'+K$ and $y'+K$, where z' is any coextensive replica of z and y' is any coextensive replica of y). M-ambiguous x is, then, to be taken as having no extension of its own. Its point is, rather, by replicating extensionally divergent replicas, to enable one sentential context to do the work of two.

To illustrate, consider the sentence-inscription:

S: Our mothers bore us.

Take the M-ambiguous 'bore' token in S as x. Now consider R and T, containing extensionally divergent replicas of x, the 'bore' token in R being z, and that in T being y.

R: Commencement speakers bore their audiences.
T: Mary and Jane bore daughters.

The pun in S consists in x's seeming to make simultaneous rival references, to birth as well as to boredom. We now relate one such apparent reference to the actual extension of z, and the other to that of y. To one putative statement made by S we associate the potential sentence $S-x+z$, and to the other we associate $S-x+y$. Rather than speaking of the *sense* of x in which it has to do with birth, we now note that x has a replica in T with the relevant extension. To read S with x taking the sense 'gave birth to' is now interpretable as reading the frame of x, i.e. $S-x$, and reading y (or any coextensive replica) in place of x.

6 A NEW PROBLEM : GREEN CENTAURS

So far, elementary ambiguity has been offered as an account of so-called type variability, and supplementary accounts have been proposed for two sorts of 'ambiguity of occurrence': the one relating to interpretive indecision (*I*-ambiguity), the other to multiple meaning (*M*-ambiguity). Is this the whole story?

Richman notes the following case, which presents a new problem. ' "Green centaur" ', he writes, 'is an ambiguous term since it may be used to mean centaurs of a certain color, or centaurs of a certain degree of experience; the classes referred to, however, are both identical, both being empty.'[15] Now imagine any two English 'green centaur' tokens, *x* and *y*. Though replicas, they are not extensionally divergent, so not *E*-ambiguous with respect to one another. Faced, moreover, with such an unlikely sentence as:

In my dream I met some experienced zebras and a green centaur,

if we cannot decide which of the above interpretations to place upon the 'green centaur' token, we can no longer explain our indecision as we earlier dealt with *I*-ambiguity. For we there required replicas of the relevant token, with divergent extensions, whereas every English replica of our undecided 'green centaur' token has the same (null) extension. Indeed, the rival interpretations of this undecided token are themselves coextensive, so the indecision cannot be attributed to variable extension.

If, thus, we find two sentences with sufficient context to resolve the indecision in question, say:

(i) There were a yellow griffin, a purple unicorn, and a green centaur at the tea party,

and

(ii) Though most of the centaurs present were well-schooled in the social graces, there was also one green centaur, whose inexperience made him visibly uncomfortable,

we still need to account for our interpreting the 'green centaur' token in (i) as differing in meaning from its replica in (ii), despite their extensional equivalence. In what does their unlikeness of meaning consist, failing elementary ambiguity?

Now the general problem of likeness of meaning (or synonymy) is the converse of the problem of ambiguity. The former concerns the conditions under which different words have the same meaning, while the latter concerns the conditions under which the same word has different meanings. While the first asks when two words have the same meaning, the second (we may say) asks when two meanings have the same word. In discussing the first problem, Nelson Goodman[16] reached the conclusion that no two words have the same meaning, but he was considering words as types. Further discussion of his ideas in papers by Richard Rudner,[17] Beverly Robbins,[18] and Goodman[19] dealt with the extension of these ideas to tokens. Since the problem of ambiguity is the reverse of that of likeness of meaning, it will be worth seeing if the inscriptional extension referred to bears on our present problem. We shall find that it does, and in unexpected ways.

7 DIFFERENCE IN MEANING

In dealing with ambiguity, we made some progress through appeal to extensional divergence, but encountered difficulty in cases where ambiguity persists without such divergence. Sameness of extension, we saw, does not in every case remove differences of meaning associated with different replicas. A parallel inadequacy forms the main problem to which Goodman's 'On Likeness of Meaning' is addressed: Sameness of extension does not guarantee sameness of meaning in the case of *words*, i.e. types. The words 'centaur' and 'unicorn', for example, differ in meaning though not in extension.

To account for this fact, Goodman proposes that it is not only the extensions of the original two words themselves that we need to consider (so-called *primary* extensions) but also the extensions of their parallel compounds (so-called *secondary* extensions). A pair of parallel compounds is formed by making an identical addition to each of the two words under consideration; thus, adding 'picture' to 'centaur' and 'unicorn', we have the parallel pair 'centaur-picture' and 'unicorn-picture'. Now, although there are neither centaurs nor unicorns, there certainly are centaur-pictures and unicorn-pictures and, moreover, they are different. Although the original words have the same extension, the parallel compounds differ in extension. Goodman's idea is, then, that the difference in meaning between two words is a matter of either their own difference in extension or that of any of their parallel compounds. In general, terms have the same meaning if and only if they have the same primary and secondary extensions.

The proposal is further generalized to cover cases in which the addition of 'picture' yields a term with null extension, e.g. 'acrid-odor-picture' and 'pungent-odor-picture' have the same (null) extension, neither applying to anything. Compounds can, however, be formed by other additions, and Goodman argues that 'description' constitutes a suffix capable of yielding all the wanted distinctions for every pair of words P and Q. For any actual inscription of the form 'a P that is not a Q' is a thing denoted by the compound 'P-description', but not by the parallel 'Q-description'. And any inscription of 'a Q that is not a P' belongs to the extension of 'Q-description' but not to that of 'P-description'. Thus, 'pungent-odor-description' and 'acrid-odor-description' differ extensionally since the first, but not the second, applies to any inscription of the form 'a pungent odor that is not an acrid odor', and vice versa. Thus, even if all pungent odors are acrid and acrid odors pungent, the terms 'pungent odor' and 'acrid odor' differ in meaning. It follows from this proposal, in fact, that 'no two different words have the same meaning'.[20]

Goodman's paper was intended to eliminate reference to images, meanings, concepts, possibilities etc., and to appeal only to the notion of extension or application to physical things. But he took the bearers of extension to be terms, i.e. word-types, although (as he later acknowledged) he would have wanted any final formulation of his proposal to admit only actual inscriptions or events, i.e. 'tokens'. What, indeed, would be the result of extending his proposal explicitly to tokens? Would it, in particular, follow that no two tokens have the same meaning? This would be even a stronger conclusion than the one suggested earlier, by the 'green centaur' example. For what the latter showed was that there are instances in which replicas differ in meaning even when they have the same extension. The conclusion that no two tokens have the same meaning clearly goes beyond the moral of the green centaurs. It implies that there is a type ambiguity that always remains even after elementary ambiguity is eliminated. Does this stronger conclusion, however, follow from Goodman's proposal reformulated for tokens?

Rudner argued that it does. In the statement S, 'A rose is a rose', the fifth word token but not the second is denoted by the term 'PS_5', defined as 'rose-description occurring in fifth place in S'. It follows, said Rudner, that the second and the fifth word token are different terms, but then, since Goodman concludes that different terms cannot have the same meaning, these tokens must differ in meaning, although they are replicas of one another.[21]

Now the above argument is vulnerable to the following criticism: While it indeed shows the first 'rose' token and the second 'rose' token in S to be different entities, it does not show that they constitute different terms or words, which would be required for them to instantiate Goodman's generalization that different *words* never have the same meaning. Rudner argues that 'PS_5' is *prima facie* a predicate of words, not mere tokens, but this seems hardly to the point. It is not the *prima facie* application of 'PS_5' that is decisive here, but rather whether the two 'rose' tokens in question can be shown to fall under Goodman's generalization, through satisfying the specific considerations upon which it is itself based. This generalization, formulated for word-types, results after all from a special argument concerning primary and secondary extensions. The question is, therefore, not whether tokens are sometimes called 'words', but rather whether this special argument can be extended to the case of tokens by independent considerations.

Such considerations are, however, not offered by Rudner. He remarks that 'if one takes simply the position that inscriptions and parts of inscriptions are meaningful, one can maintain that no "repetitive" inscription [such as "a rose is a rose"] is analytic; for no two of its constituent parts have the same primary and secondary extensions.'[22] The latter point is, however, not demonstrated by his argument. What his argument shows is that a *third* predicate, 'PS_5', has one but not the other of his 'rose' tokens in *its* extension, but it gives no reason to suppose that these two tokens themselves do not have identical extensions, both primary and secondary.

A criticism of Rudner's paper was offered by Beverly Robbins,[23] who argued not only that Rudner had failed to deduce his strong conclusion from Goodman's proposal regarding word-types, but also that the strong conclusion does not, in fact, follow. Commenting on the passage from Rudner just quoted, to the effect that no two tokens – not even coextensive replicas – have the same primary and secondary extensions, she raises the critical question as to the existence of relevant compounds of tokens, divergent parallel compounds being required for different secondary extensions. What compounds, asks Robbins, are available in the case of tokens?

Unlike a word-type, compounds of which can always be supposed (on classical platonistic assumptions) to exist, a compound of a concrete token cannot be assumed to exist; the abstract word-type is repeatable whereas the token is not. If two tokens

> themselves are to be constituents of the compounds, then they
> must actually exist or have existed as so many marks or sounds
> within these compounds. . . . In general, if we stipulate that
> the compounds corresponding to two predicate-events [tokens]
> be formed by additions to the predicate-events themselves,
> then most predicate-events, being uncompounded, will lack
> secondary extension. Among such predicate-events, those with
> identical primary extensions will be synonymous, since they
> will also have the same secondary extensions by virtue of
> having none.

Robbins thus concludes that strictly to apply Goodman's criterion of likeness of meaning to tokens yields too many synonymous pairs, 'e.g. any uncompounded "centaur"-event and "unicorn"-event, will have the same meaning.'[24]

However, we can construe the compounding of a token not as its literal embeddedness within a larger token, but rather as the embeddedness of any of its replicas therein. As Robbins puts it, we can take the statement (for tokens I_1 and C_1):

I_1 occurs in the compound C_1.

as saying:

Some replica of I_1 is part of some replica of C_1.

Such a construal obviates the difficulty that every 'centaur' token which is not literally a part of some compound must be said to have the same meaning as every such 'unicorn'-token. For we can assume, or construct at will, a suitable compound, say a 'centaur-picture' token containing a 'centaur' replica as constituent, and we can equally assume or construct a 'unicorn-picture' token containing a 'unicorn' replica as constituent. The extensional divergence of these latter compound tokens would now show a difference of meaning not only between their actual first word constituents, but also between every replica of one such constituent and every replica of the other. For by Robbins' extended notion of 'occurrence within a compound', every token occurs within every compound in which it has a replica as a constituent.

By this extended notion, however, every two tokens that are replicas of each other occur in exactly the same compounds, the *replica* relation being reflexive, symmetric, and transitive. 'Consequently', concludes Robbins, 'if two such predicate-events have the same primary extension, they will also have the same secondary extensions. The two "rose"-events in Rudner's example "A rose is a rose" will, contrary to his contention, have the same meaning.'[25] Commenting upon the Rudner-Robbins exchange in a later paper, Goodman concluded that the application of his thesis to tokens indeed does not yield the strong result that every two tokens differ in meaning, but 'only that every two word-events [tokens] that are not replicas of each other differ in meaning.'[26]

To say that no two *words* have the same meaning is a denial of synonymy. To say, further, that no two *tokens* have the same meaning is an affirmation of an ambiguity so strong as to infect *all* replica-pairs whatever. Such an affirmation would account for our 'green centaur' example by bringing it under a universal generalization: Two 'green centaur' tokens differ in meaning simply because every two tokens differ in meaning. In generalizing ambiguity for all token-pairs, however, such an account fails to explain what is peculiar to our 'green centaur' example, namely, that just those 'green centaur' replicas that involve differing interpretations are thought to differ in meaning: Two such replicas, *both* construed as indicating centaur color, will *not* be taken to differ in meaning, whereas a pair in which one indicates color and the other degree of experience *will* be supposed to involve difference in meaning. The 'green centaur' example, in other words, presents us with *particular* replica-pairs which differ in meaning even though they lack elementary ambiguity. To say that every two tokens differ in meaning is too strong a thesis to explain the particular ambiguity constituting our problem.

We have seen that this strong thesis cannot be supposed to

26

follow from Goodman's criterion. What is the state of our problem, however, if we accept Robbins's arguments? Given two replicas with identical primary extension, they cannot diverge in secondary extension since they occur in the very same compounds. It follows that every two replicas with the same primary extension *must* have the same meaning; sameness of meaning for replicas depends solely upon sameness of primary extension. And this conclusion is in direct conflict with our 'green centaur' case. For here we have replicas identical in primary extension, yet different in meaning. The situation thus turns out to be more complicated than had been supposed. Given replicas with the same primary extension, we can neither say (with Rudner) that every two of them differ in meaning, nor (with Robbins) that every two of them are alike in meaning. Some such pairs show sameness whereas some show difference. But on what does this variation depend?

8 CONSTITUENT AMBIGUITY

One idea that suggests itself immediately is to take into account the extensions of word constituents as well as compounds. Goodman's original criterion hinged on reference to the extensions of the two original words themselves, as well as the extensions of their compounds. Applied to tokens, this criterion (as we have seen) cannot account for the 'green centaur' case. But we need only note that replicas of the word constituent 'green' are characterized by elementary ambiguity, since some denote things of a certain color and others denote things of a certain degree of experience. Moreover, the particular difference of meaning characterizing 'green centaur' tokens under our two differing interpretations is exactly associated with the difference of extensional assignments to the constituent 'green' tokens in question. The upshot is, then, a revision of Goodman's original criterion to include reference to word constituents: Tokens are alike in meaning if and only if they have the same primary extensions, the same secondary extensions, and the same constituent extensions, where the latter clause is to be taken as requiring the same primary extensions for parallel word constituents.[27]

In *Languages of Art*, Goodman suggests an analogous revision of his criterion as applied to sign-types, because artificial languages may bar the free compounding characteristic of natural languages. Discussing his original criterion, he writes:[28]

> As applied to natural languages, where there is great freedom in generating compounds, this criterion tends to give the result that every two terms differ in meaning. No such result follows for more restricted languages; and indeed for these the criterion may need to be strengthened by providing further that characters differ in meaning if they are parallel compounds of terms that differ either in primary or in parallel secondary extension.

The motivation for the proposal in this passage is to provide a suitable criterion for restricted languages, whereas our present motivation has been to take account of meaning differences among replicas, which share all their compounds. But the common point is the need for a strengthening of the original criterion when limitations of one or another sort are placed on compounding. For word-types in languages with structural restrictions on compounding, reference to constituents is thus indicated. For tokens, where compounds of replicas are shared by all such replicas, compounding being thus powerless to differentiate among them, reference to constituents is equally indicated.

Once we take constituents into account, we can deal with the sort of ambiguity presented by the 'green centaur' case, a case not dealt with by Robbins's treatment. She treats replicas with identical primary extension, arguing that they cannot differ in secondary extension, i.e. cannot occur in parallel compounds with divergent extension. Our 'green centaur' case offers replicas with identical primary extension, but containing parallel constituents with differing primary extension. We have here, in other words, compounds lacking elementary ambiguity, with parallel constituents possessing elementary ambiguity. We can thus acknowledge, in extensional terms, certain differences of meaning among compound replicas with the same primary extensions. Such differences comprise what we shall refer to as *constituent ambiguity*: *x* and *y* are constituent-ambiguous relative to one another (*C*-ambiguous) when they are coextensive replicas containing parallel constituents with divergent extension.

Moreover, related to constituent ambiguity, which is another form of type variability, there is a new sort of ambiguity of occurrence: It involves indecision as to the interpretation of a single compound token, whose context is too meagre to settle the extensional alignment of a *constituent*. This notion is parallel to that of our earlier idea of *I*-ambiguity, related to elementary ambiguity of the whole. In fact, every compound predicate token which is constituent indecisive in this way (*CI*-ambiguous) contains an *I*-ambiguous constituent, and every *I*-ambiguous token renders *CI*-ambiguous any predicate compound of which it may be a part. Analogous remarks might be made with respect to compounds with *M*-ambiguous constituents, that is, compounds which are *CM*-ambiguous.

9 COMPOUND AMBIGUITY

A critical case remains, however, yet to be considered, one that is beyond the reach of any of the notions so far developed. Consider first that constituent ambiguity depends upon the separability of word constituents of given tokens. Can we not conceive of an ambiguity that remains even when such separability is not allowed? Imagine, for example, that every 'green centaur' token has been learned initially as a single indivisible unit, and that no mastery of isolated 'green' tokens has as yet been gained. It is, however, known that all 'greencentaur' tokens are identical in extension, there being no greencentaurs. Thus, there is here no elementary ambiguity, nor is there, for lack of relevant separability, any constituent ambiguity. (There can, further, be no ambiguity of occurrence in any of the forms so far distinguished.) Nevertheless, a form of ambiguity persists: the situation is here strikingly different from that involving, say, just 'unicorn' tokens, which also lack elementary as well as constituent ambiguity. What is this difference?

The contrast is seen immediately if we form compounds with 'picture' tokens in each case. All 'unicorn-picture' tokens have the same extension; on the other hand, 'greencentaur-picture' tokens are marked by elementary ambiguity: Some of these denote what, from a more sophisticated standpoint, might be described as green-colored-centaur-pictures (or pictures of green-colored centaurs), whereas others denote what, from the same standpoint, might be described as immature-centaur-pictures (or pictures of immature centaurs). Given either what sophisticates might describe as a picture of a green-colored but wordly-wise centaur, or a picture of a yellow baby centaur, it will be denoted by some but not all of the 'greencentaur-picture' replicas. The point, in short, is this: even though indivisible 'greencentaur' tokens *lack* elementary ambiguity, certain of their compounds, e.g. 'greencentaur-picture' tokens, *possess* elementary ambiguity.

Nor does this general sort of case depend upon our imagined circumstance in which the constituent of a compound ('green' in 'greencentaur') has not yet been grasped as a separable unit. Suppose two novelists use the same name 'Algernon' for their central characters in two fictional works. All replicas of the name within our given domain may then have the same (null) extension, and there are no word constituents in any of these replicas. Yet 'Algernon-description' tokens may display elementary ambiguity, some denoting portions of the one fictional work, and others denoting portions of the other. Myths employ the same name for purportedly different but actually nonexistent characters. Thus, 'The child Linus of Argos must be distinguished from Linus, the son of Ismenius, whom Heracles killed with a lyre.'[29] And Argus, the hound; Argus, son of Medea; Argus Panoptes; and Argus the Thespian are all to be distinguished[30] despite the sharing of a name with null extension and no word constituents.

Recalling Robbins's argument against the efficacy of secondary extensions to distinguish among replicas with identical primary extension, we find that she does not make this critical contrast between compounds *with*, and compounds *without*, elementary ambiguity. Concerning the two 'rose' tokens in a given 'A rose is a rose', she argues that they must occur in exactly the same compounds, since to occur in a compound (by her extended notion) is to have a replica therein. Thus, given a compound containing a replica of the one 'rose' token, this compound must also contain a replica of the other, the replica relation being transitive. 'Consequently', she concludes, 'if two such predicate-events have the same primary extension, they will also have the same secondary extensions.'[31]

Now, in any case, replicas have the same secondary extensions. But such *sameness* of secondary extensions does not imply that the extensions of the relevant compounds are the *same*. The compounds, although *shared* by all replicas of the constituents, may show extensional *divergence* amongst themselves, i.e. some may be E-ambiguous relative to others. The example Robbins deals with is one in which the relevant compounds ('rose-description' tokens) do not suggest such ambiguity, but the possibility of such ambiguity is nevertheless clear.

Consider, for example, replicas (unlike 'rose' tokens) that differ in primary extension, e.g. two tokens T_1 and T_2, of the word 'trunk', T_1 denoting containers of a certain sort and T_2 denoting certain portions of elephants. Since they are replicas, T_1 and T_2 have exactly the same secondary extensions, but such sameness clearly does not preclude elementary ambiguity of compound 'trunk-picture' tokens, some of which denote certain container-pictures but not elephant-pictures, while some do just the reverse. Since T_1 and T_2 differ in primary extension, they *ipso facto* differ in meaning, so that consideration of their compounds is, for Robbins's purposes, superfluous. But the question that concerns us here is this: Given indivisible replicas with *identical* primary extensions, does the elementary ambiguity of their shared secondary extensions contribute a new form of ambiguity to the original replicas? The 'rose' example, to be sure, does not highlight this problem, but the examples introduced in the present section do raise the issue. The 'greencentaur-picture' tokens, the 'Algernon-description' tokens, the 'Linus-description' tokens, and the 'Argus-description' tokens display elementary ambiguity despite the lack of elementary ambiguity of their respective constituents. We thus have here, it seems, another form of ambiguity, flowing inward to the constituent from elementary ambiguity of the compound; we shall refer to it as *compound ambiguity* or *K-ambiguity*.

10 MENTION-SELECTION

The notion of *K*-ambiguity diverges, however, from the conceptions hitherto introduced: it fails to associate differing extensions appropriately with the ambiguous replicas in question. If replicas R_1 and R_2 are E-ambiguous with respect to one another, they themselves differ in extension, while if they are

C-ambiguous relative to one another, some constituent of R_1 differs in extension from a parallel constituent of R_2. For K-ambiguity, we cannot say the same thing. To be sure, the compounds of R_1 and R_2 differ amongst themselves in extension, but these divergent compounds are not differentially assigned to R_1 and R_2; indeed the latter two replicas occur in all the *very same* compounds by Robbins's criterion.

It is true that extensional variation among compounds, which is here in question, has already shown itself significant in the case of non-replicas: Learning the difference in meaning between a 'centaur' token and a 'unicorn' token is *not* learning to associate different extensions with the latter pair or with their respective parallel constituents. Rather it is learning to differentiate centaur-pictures from unicorn-pictures, centaur-descriptions from unicorn-descriptions, and so forth. But then, if learning the word 'centaur' is learning how to apply also 'centaur-picture', for example, then learning the indivisible word 'greencentaur' is learning how to apply 'greencentaur-picture' as well. And if the latter is plagued by elementary ambiguity, how can learning proceed coherently?

If a child correctly withholds the term 'centaur' from everything, it may still not be clear whether the child is capable of correctly selecting centaur-pictures, and until this can be done we may be unwilling to admit that he or she has gotten the whole point. Where elementary ambiguity infects the compounds, there are, so to speak, two or more points to be gotten. We may, by subsidiary indication, help to resolve the ambiguity, limiting relevant compounds (in teaching) to certain ones with homogeneous extension, or we may expect the child to learn to vary the extension of the compounds relevantly under variation of natural context. Moreover, in gauging the child's performance, we may ourselves be undecided as to which point has been gotten, with only limited sampling of his or her wielding of compounds. Analogously, given a fragment containing the name 'Linus', we may be unable to decide whether it refers to the child Linus of Argos or to Linus the son of Ismenius, whom Heracles killed with a lyre. But 'refers' cannot here be taken as 'denotes' for in neither case is anything denoted. The question, it seems, is rather what 'Linus-description' may have denoted, for the author of the fragment in question. In our finding 'Linus' ambiguous, we are indirectly reflecting indecision as to the extension of 'Linus-description' in this context.

Still, there is a residual problem in the case of replicas, which does not arise for non-replicas. A 'centaur' token differs in meaning from a 'unicorn' token since a syntactically distinguishable group of 'centaur' compounds diverges extensionally from another such group of 'unicorn' compounds. The notion of *parallel* compounds implies that they are syntactically distinguishable and assignable to the two tokens differing in meaning. And the latter condition fails for *replicas* differing in meaning. Though extensional variation among compounds may occasion a kind of indecision respecting single tokens, disrupting learning or interpretation in the process, these varying compounds cannot be syntactically (and differentially) associated with the replicas that occasion the indecision in question; it is thus not clear what constitutes a resolution of the indecision.

Raymond, a given student of the novel, produces an 'Algernon' token, which leaves us undecided as to how he would apply the compound 'Algernon-description' – whether, in particular, he would thereby denote portions of Jones's novel or portions of Smith's. Deciding after a while in favor of Jones, we take Raymond's compound 'Algernon-description' tokens to denote portions of Jones's novel. Yet, how does this decision respecting the compound affect the status of Raymond's original 'Algernon' token? It remains as true now as before that this token occurs also in all those compounds that denote portions of Smith's novel. We have, moreover, another student, George, who also produces an 'Algernon' token and whose compound 'Algernon-description' token denotes portions of Smith's rather than Jones's novel. Let us call Raymond's 'Algernon' token A_1 and George's A_2; let us call Raymond's compound K_1 and George's K_2. K_1 and K_2 have, then, been decided to be extensionally divergent, but we want to say that this divergence of the compounds also flows inward, affecting the likeness of meaning of A_1 and A_2. We want, in short, to differentiate the latter on the basis of K_1 and K_2, but this is precisely what we cannot do, for A_1 occurs in *both* compounds, and so does A_2.

Since syntactic features are incapable of making the wanted distinctions, to associate A_1 with K_1 but not K_2, and A_2 with K_2 but not K_1 is, in effect, to presuppose a new notion of parallel compounds which cuts more finely than syntactic distinctions will allow. We have seen that, where replicas are concerned, the very notion of parallel compounds, as originally conceived, *collapses* owing to the transitivity of the replica relation. What is needed then is appeal to some notion *other than* the replica relation.

We have already spoken of learning as providing some link between token and compound; the habits governing use of the token are associated with those governing use of the compounds. To wonder whether a given 'Algernon' token is to be related to K_1 or K_2, it may now be suggested, is to wonder whether the habits governing the 'Algernon' token in question are linked through learning with habits favoring K_1 or K_2. Can this account be made more specific? Can it, moreover, be freed from its dependence on the assumption of suitable compounds available to the producers of the original tokens? In the example of the 'Linus' fragment earlier discussed, for instance, we imagined ourselves undecided as to whether the name referred to the child Linus of Argos or to Linus the son of Ismenius, and we characterized such indecision as concerning the denotation of 'Linus-description' for the author of the fragment in question. But there may have been no such compound in the author's context and to talk, therefore, of linking his 'Linus' habits with his 'Linus-description' habits would thus be artificial.

A further consideration of the learning situation provides us with a clue. We noted that a child who has withheld the term 'centaur' from everything is still not judged to have gotten the whole point until we are confident he or she can correctly select centaur-pictures. Now in the selection of such pictures, the child does not, in fact, typically use the compound 'centaur-picture', but rather the original term 'centaur'. Moreover, pointing out the centaur *in* a given picture, the child is expected to apply the same term 'centaur' to some appropriate region of the picture. Such quasi-denotative uses of the term we shall call *mention-selective*, for, though literally denoting neither centaur-pictures nor centaur-regions, it is here employed, in a manner reminiscent of metaphor, so as to select centaur-mentions in fact. In the case of 'centaur', which has null (literal) denotation, its mention-selective employment may well be related to learning this denotation itself.

Mention-selective use is limited, however, neither to centaur-pictures nor children. A child is often asked to point out trees, dogs, and automobiles in picture books and magazines. And in our own typical labeling of a picture of a man 'Man' (rather than 'Man-picture'), we ourselves apply the term 'Man' to select not a man but a picture; we here apply the term not to what it denotes but rather to a mention thereof. Logicians have warned us so vehemently against confusing use with mention that we tend to overlook this employment of terms in the course of learning and in subsequent linguistic practice. Denotative and mention-selective uses are, I suggest, in fact intimately related, the one sometimes guiding the learning of the other and vice versa, the process resembling in significant ways the transfer phenomena characteristic of metaphor.

Consider the relation between the word 'man' and man-pictures; the word is used not only to select men but to sort pictures of men. 'Man' literally denotes men and 'man-picture' literally denotes man-pictures, but 'man' is also transferred and applied mention-selectively to man-pictures. If a person has mastered the conventional use of the term 'man', he is normally expected to employ it properly not only in pointing out men but also in selecting man-pictures, and man-regions within such pictures. The habits governing his employment of 'man' tokens in application to men are supposed, that is, to guide (and perhaps be guided by) his application of such tokens to man-mentions.[32]

Returning now to Raymond and George, the difference in meaning of their respective 'Algernon' tokens does not lie in their primary extensions but rather in their mention-selective applications. That is to say, A_1 mention-selects the extension of K_1; and A_2 mention-selects the extension of K_2. Given a portion of Jones's novel, or a suitable portrait of its hero, we ask whether Raymond's or George's 'Algernon' token applies to it by way of mention-selective transfer. Our indecision with respect to the 'Linus' fragment, similarly, is an indecision as to what descriptions or pictures or other portrayals are mention-selected by its constituent 'Linus' token. We ask, in effect, what mentions the habits of the token's producer select as suitable for labeling by the token in question, or replicas thereof. Analogously, too, for our indivisible 'greencentaur' tokens; though lacking elementary ambiguity, they may vary in what they mention-select.

K-ambiguity, initially introduced as consisting in elementary ambiguity of secondary extension (i.e. of compounds), may thus be reformulated as variation in mention-selection characterizing the original tokens themselves. Replicas may vary in mention-selection despite their syntactical indistinguishability; we may estimate one, but not another, to be linked through mention-selection with some particular extension of an ambiguous compound of our construction. One non-compound replica may then, indeed, differ in meaning from another with the same primary extension, through differing in its mention-selection.[33] If it be said that the concept of K-ambiguity depends still for its initial *explanation* on the notion of extensionally divergent *compounds*, it is nevertheless not presupposed that either the concept or its explanation is shared by producers of the replicas we are concerned to interpret. *We* may judge by means of compounds available to us; we need not also attribute knowledge or employment of these compounds to the users whose replicas are in question. Yet, we may conclude that the extensional divergence represented by such compounds flows inward to differentiate the meanings of constituent replicas.

II

VAGUENESS

Vagueness is a challenge to the theory of language. On the one hand there is little or no agreement on such elementary matters as the vehicle and domain of vagueness, the opposite of vagueness, the relations among vagueness, ambiguity, and generality – and still others. On the other hand, large theses have been propounded concerning the methodological, logical, and ontological status of vagueness, for example, that vagueness is a universal characteristic of descriptive terms, that it is in fundamental conflict with standard logic, that it shows some basic limitation of the human mind or derives from an ineradicable blur in nature. Vagueness has, moreover, been associated with a variety of forms of indeterminacy, and concomitant interpretations have often harbored both surface difficulties and deep philosophical troubles.

Let us begin our present inquiry by recalling a distinction already introduced, between elementary ambiguity and vagueness – taking the latter as an indeterminacy or ambivalence in deciding the applicability of a term to an object. A token x is E-ambiguous within D if it has a replica y in D such that x and y are extensionally divergent. A given token may thus be E-unambiguous relative to a specified domain either in having no replicas therein or in having only such as are coextensive – and yet it may be vague, that is, characterized by ambivalence as to its applicability to an object under consideration. The vagueness of a token does not, in other words, presuppose that it diverge in extension from a replica of itself. Conversely, that x and y are E-ambiguous relative to one another does not imply that either is inadequately decidable in application to any relevant object, as the example of indicator terms shows.

Noting that E-ambiguity consists in extensional variation among replicas, each of which may nevertheless be perfectly definite in application, we sought further to account for the indecision often imputed to the single token in describing an expression as 'ambiguous'. And we rejected the idea of identifying such indecision – related to ambiguity – with the indecision of mere vagueness. The required notion of the former indecision, we reflected, had to be related suitably to type variability, i.e. to extensional change across replicas – it could not be mere indecision, pure and simple. In Richman's terms, earlier cited, the 'psychological ambiguity' of the token had to be construed as involving 'semantical ambiguity', that is to say, possession of more than one meaning by the type.[1]

Thus we were prompted to introduce the notion of I-ambiguity, taking token x (within context C) as I-ambiguous, relative to C, when (roughly) x's coextensiveness with one or another of its mutually E-ambiguous replicas z and y is required – but not further decided – by C. The I-ambiguous x (relative to C) is thus characterized by indecision with respect to its alignment with z or with y.

Do we, then, need to reckon with two discrete sorts of indecision – one (associated with vagueness) pertaining to the applicability of a token to an object, and the other (associated with I-ambiguity) pertaining to the extensional alignment of a token with one or another of its divergent replicas? The answer is negative since the latter sort is included in the former. For if divergent replicas z and y are rivals for extensional alignment with an I-ambiguous x, there must be some object respecting which the applicability of x is undecided, even if discrete from the object o to which x may be attributed in the context in question. Indecision as to whether the boundaries of x's extension coincide with those of z or of y in fact affects the applicability of x to all those objects with respect to which z and y diverge. I-ambiguity seems thus interpretable as a special case of vagueness (i.e. indecision over application of a term to objects), rather than vagueness being (as some have suggested) a species of ambiguity.

That I-ambiguity is a special case may be shown by the peculiar constraints imposed on the resolution of its indecision. Consider, to begin with, a token x, not I-ambiguous but nevertheless vague relative to objects within our sphere of consideration, S. S contains, we suppose: (i) objects to which x decidably applies, (ii) objects to which x decidably fails to apply, and (iii) objects to which x neither decidably applies nor decidably fails to apply. These circumstances leave further inquiry unconstrained as to how the indecision may be resolved. In particular, we are prepared to envisage all objects within category (iii) as newly assigned to the clear positive category (i), or else as newly assigned to the clear negative category (ii).

Contrast, now, the case of I-ambiguity, where token x' is undecided as to its alignment with mutually divergent replicas z and y. Suppose the latter replicas to have overlapping extensions. Some objects are, then, (i') denoted by both z and y; other objects are, we suppose, (ii') denoted by neither, while others still are (iii') denoted by one or the other alone. Assume further, for simplicity's sake, that neither z nor y is vague relative to our sphere of consideration.

Now x' is coextensive with z or with y but undecided as to which. Thus it applies, in any case, to the objects of category (i') and fails to apply, in any event, to the objects of category (ii'). It is objects of category (iii') that fall within the region of indecision of x'. But resolution of such indecision is not, as before, unconstrained. For if all objects of (iii') are assigned to x''s positive category, x' will apply *both* to things denoted by z but not by y, *and* to those denoted by y but not by z; it will thus be coextensive neither with z nor with y. Analogously, if (iii') is wholly assigned to x''s negative category, x' will be withheld from every object that is z but not y (hence failing of coextensiveness with z) *and* withheld also from everything that is y but not z (hence failing of coextensiveness with y). Whatever resolution is provided for x', it will need to draw a line within the region of indecision (iii'), separating elements denoted by z but not y from those denoted by y but not z.

To illustrate, let x' be the 'is gold' token in a particular sentence replica of:

That piece of cloth is gold,

within a specified context C. The indecision over x' is whether to take it as coextensive with a particular one of its replicas z which denotes things made of gold, or rather as coextensive with another replica y, denoting things of bright yellow color.

Table 1

	Bright yellow (denoted by y)	Not bright yellow (not denoted by y)
Made of gold (denoted by z)	(i')	(iii'b)
Not made of gold (not denoted by z)	(iii'a)	(ii')

Safely applying x' to things that are both bright yellow and made of gold [(i') in Table 1], and safely withholding it from things that are neither [(ii') in Table 1], we cannot decide whether it applies to all bright yellow things or to all things made of gold. The undecided elements fall into the two groups (iii'a) and (iii'b) of Table 1. If we now assign both of these groups to x''s positive category, x' will apply to some things not bright yellow (not denoted by y) and also to some things not made of gold (not denoted by z); that is – it will be coextensive neither with y nor with z. Similarly, if we assign both (iii'a) and (iii'b) to the negative category of x', x' will be withheld from some things made of gold and from some bright yellow things; again it will be coextensive neither with z nor with y. Any resolution of the indecision in question will need to keep (iii'a) separate from (iii'b). *I*-ambiguity is thus seen as a species of vagueness, the resolution of which obeys special restrictions, its indecision being channeled into certain paths from the outset.

2 VAGUENESS, GENERALITY, PRECISION

Vagueness, as treated thus far, is independent of generality.[2] A general term may be clearly decidable in its application to every object within the domain of our consideration. That one term, e.g. 'animal', is more general than another, e.g. 'kangaroo', in applying to everything denoted by the latter and to other things besides, does not argue that it is more vague; both terms may be clearly decidable within the domain in question. It is, of course, true that the less general of a pair of terms, e.g. 'chair', may be clearly decidable in a given domain for which the more general 'article of furniture' may be ambivalent relative to some objects therein. But it may also happen that the less general of a pair of terms may be vague where the more general term is not. I may be unable to decide whether to call something 'a tree' (though small) or 'not a tree but a bush', and yet be perfectly clear that it is an instance of 'living thing', even though 'living thing' is more general than 'tree'.

A singular term (lacking generality altogether) may yet be thoroughly undecidable in a given domain; with neither clear positive nor clear negative denotata, all elements of the domain may be absorbed into its region of indecision. By contrast, a maximally general term, e.g. 'is self-identical', may utterly lack vagueness. A term and its negate must be equal in vagueness relative to any domain, since any element undecidable for one is undecidable for the other; by contrast, a term may be considered to vary from its negate in generality. Thus, for the domain of all physical things, 'inanimate' may be judged more general than 'animate' despite the fact that they are of equivalent vagueness. And 'is self-identical', which altogether lacks vagueness, is equivalent in this regard to 'is non-self-identical' although the former denotes everything and the latter nothing.

The independence of vagueness from generality implies that the widespread contrast of vagueness with specificity (or precision) cannot be upheld in fact. To take our earlier example, 'living thing' is more general than 'tree'; to call something 'a living thing' affords a less specific or precise description of it than calling it 'a tree'. Yet, the more precise term may also be the more vague. Every object within some particular domain, as we have earlier seen, may be clearly decidable as being a living thing or not, whereas some objects in the domain may not be clearly decidable as being trees or not. It is easier to judge that a shelf is *roughly* two feet long than to judge it to be *precisely* two feet long.

Suppose we have three color terms, 'red', 'yellow', and 'blue', and apply them to a domain of colored surfaces in which the number of undecidable cases is negligible. If we increase the precision of our color vocabulary, distinguishing several varieties among the red surfaces, the yellow surfaces, and the blue surfaces and adding new terms for surfaces falling between these three groups in color, the effect of such increase in precision may well be an increase in the number of undecidable cases as well. Asked to classify several lines by means of the terms 'less than or equal to one inch in length', 'from two to three inches in length' and 'from four to five inches in length', we may find no undecidable lines in our given domain. Yet the same domain may give rise to undecidable cases if we elaborate our vocabulary to register finer distinctions, e.g. 'equal to or less than $\frac{1}{4}$ inch in length', 'from $\frac{1}{2}$ to $\frac{3}{4}$ inch in length', 'from 1 inch to $1\frac{1}{4}$ inches in length', etc. In cases such as these, the more precise our descriptive vocabulary, the more difficult it seems to become to make the discriminations demanded for its application. It is, moreover, always possible to define mathematical distinctions beyond the reach of our discriminatory apparatus, no matter how powerful this apparatus may be. The upshot is that we may increase vagueness by increasing precision and decrease vagueness by diminishing precision. The reduction of vagueness and the reduction of imprecision are often in conflict and they cannot, in general, be maximized together.[3]

We began by suggesting the *independence* of vagueness from generality; now our examples seem to yield the stronger suggestion of *inverse variation*. Yet if vagueness and generality do not vary directly, neither do they vary inversely. Recall our earlier case of 'chair', a term that may in certain domains be both less general and less vague than 'article of furniture.' Note further that even the domains of color and length, which afforded us clear inverse examples, do not show a *uniformly* inverse relation between vagueness and generality. Certain increments of precision yield no increments of vagueness at all for given domains. An object undecidable as between 'red' and 'yellow' is likely to remain thus, but not to become more, undecidable with the addition of 'purple' to the vocabulary; it may even become a decided case with the addition of 'orange'. A set of surfaces all decidable as instances of 'white' or 'red' will be likely to remain decidable after the addition of 'green'. Similarly, lines readily classifiable under the terms 'less than or equal to one inch' and 'between a foot and two feet in length' will be likely to remain thus decidable after we add the term 'between 5 and $5\frac{1}{4}$ inches long'.

We conclude, thus, that vagueness is independent of generality, showing neither regular direct, nor regular inverse, variation with it. The opposite of vagueness is, in any case, not specificity or precision; to eliminate imprecision may be to increase vagueness as well. This general conclusion seems natural in view of the interpretation here given to vagueness, i.e. an ambivalence or indeterminacy in deciding the applicability of a term. For vagueness, taken thus, is a pragmatic notion variable with person (and time); there seems no reason to expect the semantic notion of generality to be regularly related to it.

3   VAGUENESS AND MOLECULAR COMPOUNDS

We consider now the relation of vagueness to compounding: What is the connection, if any, between a term and its compounds with respect to vagueness? It is clear, first of all, that vagueness is not transmitted in every case from word-constituent to containing sentence. That 'mountain' is vague relative to a given domain does not preclude the decidability of 'Some mountains are snow-capped' as a truth concerning that domain, nor, certainly, does it prevent easy decidability of 'All mountains are mountains' or 'If mountains are sonnets, then birds are windows'. Conversely, sentences that are not easily decidable do not in every case contain vague constituent terms; they may, for example, be merely excessively long or excessively complex, even if theoretically decidable. Consider the sentence: 'Given that if the birds sing only if the stars are bright then the sun shines, then if it is not the case that if the stars are bright then the sun shines then the birds don't sing.' Here the terms are relatively free of vagueness while the nesting of conditionals reduces easy decidability for the ordinary reader. And the fact that a serious assertion such as Fermat's Last Theorem has, without undue length or complexity, defied efforts at proof for so long in no way argues that any of its constituent terms is vague. Nor is the vagueness of a constituent indicated by my inability to decide the truth of 'There is a man in Oshkosh over seven and one half feet tall.'

We turn now to non-sentential compounds of terms, and consider first *molecular* compounds, that is, compounds interpretable as resulting from application of logical (i.e. truth-functional or quantificational) operations to their components. Will the vagueness of such a component carry over to every molecular compound in which it is embedded? Clearly not. Imagine a domain in which 'yellow' is vague, owing solely to its ambivalence relative to a certain element, say a cube. Then 'yellow ball' may not be vague at all, for every element may be clearly decidable as a ball or not, and every ball will, by hypothesis, be clearly decidable as yellow or not; moreover, the compound is not likely to cause trouble on account of excessive length or complexity.

Even if *every* component term of a molecular compound is vague, the compound may not be, since the respective undecidable regions of the components may diverge, each clearly falling into the complement of the other term. Thus, 'blue' may be vague in a given domain because ambivalent just with respect to a and b, and 'heavy' may also be vague in that domain because ambivalent just with respect to c and d. We now suppose that c and d are clearly non-blue, while a and b are clearly non-heavy. Then 'blue and heavy' will be likely to be non-vague in the domain in question. For it will be clearly withheld from a and b, since these are clearly non-heavy, and also from c and d, since these are clearly non-blue. All other objects in the domain will then be (i) clearly blue and clearly heavy, (ii) clearly blue and clearly not heavy, (iii) clearly heavy and clearly not blue, or (iv) clearly neither. The compound in question will now be clearly applicable to objects of the first variety, (i), and clearly non-applicable to the rest (see Table 2).

Table 2

	Blue	?Blue?	Non-blue
Heavy	(i)	o	(iii)
?Heavy?	o	o	c,d
Non-heavy	(ii)	a,b	(iv)

We consider now the converse: Will the vagueness of a molecular compound carry over to every one of its component terms? Recall again our domain in which 'yellow' is vague

44

because of its ambivalence just with respect to a given cubical element. In this domain the compound 'yellow cube' will also be vague, even if 'cube' is altogether free of vagueness. The vagueness of a molecular compound is thus not always paralleled by vagueness in *each* of its component terms.

Does the vagueness of such a compound require, however, that at least one component term be vague? Since a molecular compound may have any (finite) number of components, easy decidability will lapse for such compounds beyond a certain length or degree of complexity, in any case. Thus, the vagueness of the compound does not, in general, require that at least one of its components be vague.

Moreover, even a short and simple compound lacking vague components may defy easy decidability as a whole, e.g. 'man without a brother'. And if I find the *sentence* 'There is a man in Oshkosh over seven and one half feet tall' undecidable, I will find the *non-sentential-compound* 'is a cube and there is a man in Oshkosh over seven and one half feet tall' no more decidable.

4 VAGUENESS, ATOMIC COMPOUNDS AND MENTION-SELECTION

We consider now those non-sentential compounds that are *atomic* rather than molecular, that is, interpretable rather as single units than as logical functions of their components. Thus 'little elephant' is atomic since (at least some) little elephants are not little, and 'witch hunter' is atomic since no witch hunter is a witch and many are, moreover, not hunters. 'Picture of a griffin' expresses no relation to such things as griffins, there being none; 'picture of a cow' does not convey a relation to some particular (though unspecified) *x*, such that *x* is a cow, although there *are* plenty of cows. Both of the latter compounds are atomic, and best supplanted, respectively, by 'griffin-picture' and 'cow-picture', to break the analogy with relational expressions.

Will the vagueness of an atomic compound now carry over to its components? Clearly not. 'Little elephant' may be vague relative to a domain for which neither 'little' nor 'elephant' is vague. 'Witch hunter' may, analogously, be vague where neither of its components is, and similar remarks hold for 'cow-picture' and 'painting of a unicorn'. Will the vagueness of a component, conversely, imply the vagueness of every one of its atomic compounds? The answer is again negative, for, to take the reverse of our earlier example, 'little' may be vague relative to a domain for which 'little elephant' may be free of vagueness. Consider another instance: there may be no question that a given snapshot is a picture of Uncle George (whom we have never met), but we may falter before the task of identifying him in the flesh.

The latter case is worth special notice, since it touches on the relation between a term ('Uncle George') and an atomic compound ('Uncle George-picture') denoting Uncle George-mentions. As suggested in our earlier discussion of ambiguity, a term serves not only to denote what it mentions but also to select appropriate parallel mentions. Thus, 'tree' denotes trees but mention-selects tree-pictures and tree-descriptions; 'centaur' denotes nothing, but mention-selects centaur-pictures and centaur-regions within centaur-pictures. Our earlier discussion suggested also that denotation and mention-selection are psychologically related in intimate ways, the one sometimes guiding the other and vice versa, the process resembling metaphoric transfer.

Where a term (e.g. 'centaur') has null denotation, its mention-selective use may, evidently, help in the learning of this very fact; denoting nothing, the term yet mention-selects an array of depictions and descriptions to which no entity (empirically) answers. Moreover, for any term, we normally think of its mastery as embracing not only denotative but mention-selective capacities as well. Denoting men, 'man' is normally expected to serve also in the (mention-selective) captioning of man-pictures. This double role of the term, by which it is linked not only to its denotata but also to allied mentions, serves to develop, or to strengthen, a family of representations for a given range of objects.

I conjecture that in the beginning was confusion of words and things, a mixture of use and mention. Psychologists and anthropologists have taught us about a variety of related phenomena, e.g. attribution of causal powers to words, fears related to words, word magic, etc. These phenomena may perhaps be grouped under the general idea of confusion of denotation with mention-selection, the creation of a family of representations in which each term indifferently refers to its instances and, concurrently, to its companion signs.[4] Thus 'tree' refers to trees but also to tree-pictures and to 'tree's. No wonder that in the child's world, symbols take on the features and powers of reality. With the dawning of the fundamental distinction between denotation and mention-selection, I further imagine, come various devices for fixing it in mind – including the use of explicit compounds of terms to denote their respective ranges of mention-selection. 'Picture of a tree', 'tree-picture', and 'tree-description', for example, come to supplant 'tree' itself in reference to tree-mentions when theoretical clarity is important, and denotation alone now suffices, without mention-selection, to make the appropriate distinctions. Of course, mention-selection persists, as I have urged, but it is recognized as a function different from denotation and it is avoidable through recourse to suitable compounds.

Now we have seen above that the vagueness of an atomic compound and the vagueness of its components are not regularly related. Nevertheless we may, where the compound denotes mentions of certain sorts, employ it to help reduce the relative vagueness of a component, or vice versa. Preparing a child for Uncle George's visit, we may refer him to a snapshot we call 'a picture of Uncle George', hoping that the non-vagueness of the latter term may help to decrease the vagueness of 'Uncle George' when the visit takes place. Similarly, people prepare for tours by looking at guide book illustrations, and medical students are taught about rare diseases by being shown photographs of their victims. In all these cases, we hope the non-vagueness of the atomic compounds may help to decrease the vagueness of the components, relying here typically, as we do, on some grasp of the general conventions of picturing.

Conversely, we may initially rely on the non-vagueness of components in reducing the vagueness of certain atomic compounds, and thus in developing a general grasp of a family of mentions. Familiarity with objects of various sorts and facility in typical ways of denoting them may be used as a base for acquiring abilities to recognize and denote certain of their representations. Both processes may, further, be variously intertwined. Learning to 'read' photographs, given initial recognition of the people they represent (or mention), we may then use photographs of hitherto unknown persons as aids to recognizing them upon first appearance. Learning to recognize fractured bones with the help of X-ray representations of them, we may expand our competence in identifying allied representations of other disabilities.

How, it may be asked, is this process possible? 'Uncle George' is after all not a logical constituent of the atomic 'Uncle George-picture'. How, then, can the non-vagueness of the former help the child to acquire a competence to wield the latter? How, conversely, may the non-vagueness of 'Uncle George-picture' aid in reducing the vagueness of 'Uncle George'?

It is, first of all, important to note that structure is not exclusively logical. The presupposition of the question is that atomic compounds, not being logical functions of their components, lack the structure required to make the relevant learning comprehensible. This presupposition is, however, groundless. There is no reason to suppose that logical decomposition has any special primacy with respect to the issues of learning that concern us here.[5] The term 'Uncle George' is after all, a syntactic component of 'Uncle George-picture'; every 'Uncle George-picture'-inscription (speaking strictly) contains, as an initial segment, a word compound, comprising a replica of every 'Uncle-George'-inscription.

Secondly, the term 'Uncle George' not only denotes but mention-selects. I have suggested that the very distinction between the two functions is initially unmarked, application of a term being made indifferently to instances as well as to parallel mentions, and only later becoming crystallized and reflective. In any case the application to mentions may be considered akin to metaphoric transfer: 'zebra' does not take zebra-pictures as instances, but forced onto a given realm of pictorial mentions, it will, with relative determinacy, select (and help to define) zebra-pictures in fact. The direction of transfer here is from *denotation* to *selection*. Now the elements thus *selected* by the term 'zebra' are in turn *denoted* by the atomic compound 'zebra-picture'. The compound is thus rendered less vague through the intermediary, transferred action of mention-selection by the component term.

Conversely, 'zebra-picture' may be transferred to real zebras, the representation helping to form a determinate and appropriate selection of animals. This process may be conceived as one in which 'zebra' initially mention-selects a certain array of pictures, and is then forced onto the animal realm, where no mentions are found. Here we find the denotation of instances following the lead of mention-selection, the total process again helping to refine the very distinction itself. The reduction of vagueness in the component by the atomic compound may thus be associated with the reverse transfer from *selection* to *denotation* by the component term.

5 RELATIVITY AND THE UNIVERSALITY OF VAGUENESS

It is time to make explicit the multiple relativity of vagueness. The impression is sometimes conveyed that vagueness is a property of the term itself, but this is certainly an oversimplification. We have already remarked that, taken as an ambivalence in deciding a term's application, vagueness varies with person and time. So construed, it is also variable with assumed domain of elements as well as with various circumstances of the decision task. Generally speaking, vagueness is relative to term, domain, decision task, person, and time. An alteration in any of these factors, holding the rest constant, may in certain cases produce vagueness where none had existed before or eliminate the vagueness that had been present earlier. Illustrations of this generalization will come readily to mind.

It has often been asserted that vagueness is a universal property of descriptive, or empirical, terms. This assertion of universality, however, requires reconsideration in view of the relativity just noted. M. Black, for example, writes, 'It is claimed that all symbols whose application involves the recognition of sensible qualities are vague . . .'.[6] Taking color as his illustrative sensible realm, he points to the continuity of change in hues ordered by least perceptible differences as creating borderline uncertainties in the application of color names. All descriptive or ' "material" terms', Black concludes, 'all whose application requires the recognition of the presence of sensible qualities, are vague in the sense described.'[7]

There is a distinction, however, between the mere involvement of sensory recognition in the application of a term and the availability of elements, perceivable by the senses, to which the term is only ambivalently applicable. A term whose application uniformly 'involves the use of the senses' (in Black's phrase)[8] will yet be variably ambivalent, depending, in part, upon the domain in question. The term 'horse', though requiring sensory capacities in its application, may be applied without any ambivalence by a child within the domain of familiar physical objects in its home environment. An expansion of this domain occasioned by a visit to the zoo may produce a new ambivalence for the child, i.e. whether to apply the term in question to the zebra or rather to withhold it. Relative to the initial, familiar domain, 'horse' is not vague for this child; relative to the expanded domain, it is.

Domain, then, makes a difference; it cannot be held that every descriptive term is vague relative to every domain. Nor is a defense of the latter thesis to be found in appeal to *possible objects*, for instance, in the suggestion that the child's initial domain be construed to contain, if not an actual, then at least a possible zebra. For in the first place, the initial domain envisaged is, by hypothesis, restricted to (actual) objects in the child's surroundings; to add so-called possible objects changes the example, thus failing to establish the universality thesis in question. In the second place, possible objects are wrapped in obscurity; to rest any thesis upon them is as good as surrendering the thesis altogether. In the third place, assuming some sense to be given to the admission of possible zebras to the domain in question, would vagueness be thereby guaranteed? Even a child undecided as to whether or not a zebra is a horse may be clear that a *possible zebra*, whatever it may be thought to be, is at any rate not a horse.

6   THE POSSIBILITY OF VAGUENESS

In defense of universality, it may rather be suggested that for any domain free of vagueness for a given term, it is possible to supplement that domain by relevant borderline elements, thus introducing vagueness in the enlarged domain. Universality, interpreted thus, relates not to *vagueness* but to the *possibility of vagueness*. The latter notion has been discussed by Waismann under the label 'open texture'.[9] A descriptive term, even if not vague relative to a given domain, has open texture in that some enlarged domain may be envisaged in which the term in question is indeed vague. The point of the universality thesis, as presently understood, is not that vagueness is never eliminable, but rather that it is always producible. It is open texture that is never eliminable.

How are we, however, to understand the *possible enlargement of a domain* or the *envisagement of added borderline elements* for the term in question? One interpretation that suggests itself is the following: (i) There are in fact borderline objects for any term, inclusion of which within a domain renders the term vague for that domain. Thus, for any domain D relative to which a term t is non-vague, there is another, D', comprising D plus at least one borderline object of t, such that t is vague relative to D'. The present universality thesis thus claims not that every descriptive term is vague relative to *every* domain, but rather that every descriptive term is vague relative to *some* domain. A weaker variant of the present version is (i)': There may in fact exist, so far as we know, borderline objects for any term whatever; thus every descriptive term *may*, so far as we know, be vague relative to some domain.

A different interpretation is the following: (ii) We may conceive or describe or imagine borderline elements for any descriptive term which, were they to exist, would render the term vague relative to any domain containing them. It is not here claimed that such borderline objects do exist, nor, even, that their existence is compatible with our present knowledge. The claim is only that they are conceivable or describable or thinkable. When Waismann speaks of a cat that 'grew to a gigantic size . . . . or could be revived from death',[10] he is neither asserting its existence as a borderline case of 'cat' nor denying that contemporary knowledge rules out such existence. He wants only to show 'that we can think of situations in which we couldn't be certain whether something was a cat or some other animal (or a *jinni*).'[11]

7 OPEN TEXTURE, COMPOUNDS AND MENTION-SELECTION

Let us address ourselves to the latter interpretation (ii) first. It will of course not do to admit such an interpretation if it reverts to the serious postulation of possible entities – if, that is to say, it holds 'cat' to be of open texture since vague relative to a domain containing a *possible cat* of gigantic size. Possible borderline objects, introduced to show universal open texture rather than, as before, universal vagueness, result anyhow in the same notorious obscurities. Since, moreover, it may be reasoned that a possible cat is no cat at all, 'cat' is not undecided relative to a possible gigantic cat, even assuming the (misguided) postulation of the latter. The wanted indecision, to be relevant at all, would need to be taken subjunctively – i.e. the indecision would be expected to arise were the possible borderline elements realized in fact. To the pains of possibility are thus added the sorrows of the subjunctive.

If talk of possible objects is in any case to be excluded, is there another way of making sense of interpretation (ii)? If the conceivability of a gigantic cat is not to involve postulation of a possible gigantic cat, does the interpretation in question need to be wholly surrendered? The answer is no, for (as we have already intimated in our earlier discussions of compounds)[12] the point of putative reference to possible borderline objects may be alternatively expressed in terms of actual representations (e.g. pictures, descriptions) of relevant sorts.

Thus, having mastered the use of 'cat' in application to familiar things, we may be undecided as to whether to apply 'picture of a cat' to the painting of a cat-like creature depicted as standing higher than the Empire State Building. A child who has no difficulty applying the term 'horse' within its familiar surroundings may yet puzzle (as in our earlier example) over the question whether to apply the term to the first live zebra encountered in the zoo. But even prior to the zoo visit, the same child may be baffled as to whether or not to *caption* the *picture of a zebra* 'horse', using the latter term now not to denote, but to select horse-mentions. Or – what comes to the same thing – the child may be undecided as to whether or not to denote the picture by the compound phrase 'picture of a horse'. Similarly, a child may be uncertain as to whether the characterization, 'animal shaped like a horse but with striped skin', encountered in a story, is a *description of a horse* or not.

The thesis of universal open texture under interpretation (ii) may thus be restated, without purported reference to possible objects and without subjunctive appeal to their hypothetical realization, as follows: Every descriptive term has some compound with '-picture' or '-description' or '-representation' which is vague relative to some domain. To illustrate, 'cat' is open textured since the compound phrase 'description of a cat' is vague relative to any domain containing the characterization 'animal anatomically like a cat but capable of being revived from death.' Open texture hinges thus not on the hypothetical expansion of a term's given domain or its putative reference to possibles, but rather on the uncertainty with which its mention-denoting compounds apply to actual things. Alternatively, the universality thesis may be expressed as follows: Every descriptive term is uncertain with respect to its mention-selection of some object. The ambivalence of the term itself in captioning pictures, for example, is here taken as a facet of open texture. In this version as well, open texture is expressed without appeal to possibility or the subjunctive, resting solely on the mention-selective relation of the term itself to actual things.

8   OPEN TEXTURE AND ANALYTICITY

The construal of open texture in terms of representations, as just explained, may be thought relevant to the interpretation of analyticity: The question whether 'animal shaped like a cat but standing four storeys high' is a cat-description or not may be related to such questions as whether or not a cat *might* stand four storeys high, whether it is just *contingently* true that cats do not stand four storeys high (and not *necessarily* so), whether – in particular – it is *synthetic*, rather than *analytic*, that no cat stands four storeys high. A subject's willingness to call the above descriptive phrase a cat-description would, according to the proposal suggested, be counted in favor of his affirmative attitude to the three latter questions; his unwillingness would be held indicative of a negative attitude. In general, a subject's deployment of relevant mention-denoting compounds of a term might be said to represent his division of true statements involving the term into analytic and synthetic truths. And open texture – i.e. the vagueness of relevant compounds – would reflect a gap in such division.

An analogous suggestion for the use of representations (in the context of a defense of intensions rather than a discussion of vagueness) is made by Rudolf Carnap, who expresses it, however, in terms of *possibility*.[13] Considering the case of a German speaker whose linguistic behavior is under investigation, Carnap asks how one might decide between two rival dictionary entries purporting to state the subject's understanding of the word *Pferd*:

(1) *Pferd*, horse
(2) *Pferd*, horse or unicorn.

Since the extensions of 'horse' and 'horse or unicorn' are identical, no response by the subject to any actual thing can differentiate between (1) and (2). What else, asks Carnap, is there for the linguist to investigate beyond the subject's responses as to the applicability of *Pferd* to all actual objects? 'The answer is', writes Carnap, 'he must take into account not only the actual cases, but also possible cases.'[14] Carnap sees no objection to the linguist's questioning the subject with the aid of such modal expressions as e.g. 'possible case' etc. On the other hand, he does not suppose such questioning to be necessary, since the linguist may also question the subject with the help of suitable representations, leaving it undecided whether these are satisfied by any objects or not. As relevant representations, Carnap suggests such a *description* as the German equivalent of 'a thing similar to a horse, but having only one horn in the middle of the forehead', and a *picture* of a unicorn. Having produced the description or the picture, the linguist is then, according to Carnap, to ask the subject 'whether he is willing to apply the word "Pferd" to a thing of this kind', a yes confirming (2), a no confirming (1).[15]

The latter question is taken by Carnap to query the subject's willingness to apply the term to a *possible case* indicated by the representation. Even if the linguist does not use modal language, the intent of the question for Carnap is modal or, at any rate, subjunctive. That is, an affirmative answer must be construed as saying, 'If there *were* a horselike, one-horned animal, it *would* be denoted by "Pferd"', rather than 'If there *is* a horselike, one-horned animal, it *is* denoted by "Pferd"'. For, given a subject who knows there are no unicorns, the latter affirmative response to the question does *not* confirm (2) as against (1), for it is perfectly consistent with (1).

We have, however, seen how a procedure such as Carnap's is interpretable without appeal to possibles or the use of subjunctive expressions – descriptions and pictures being themselves actual rather than possible objects. Asking the subject whether he is willing to apply 'Pferd' to a (possible) thing of the kind indicated by a given picture may, as we have seen, better be construed as asking him whether he is willing to apply the compound 'Pferd-picture' to the picture itself, or (alternatively) whether he is prepared to caption the picture 'Pferd'. We have also shown how to construe open texture as ambivalent application of a term's compounds or as its ambivalent mention-selection.

Appealing rather to intensions defined in terms of possibility, (taking the intension of a predicate 'as its range, which comprehends those possible kinds of objects for which the predicate holds') Carnap describes the phenomenon of open texture as 'intensional vagueness'. Taking the word 'Mensch' as an example, he suggests that, whereas the extensional vagueness of this word is relatively small for a typical subject, its intensional vagueness is, by contrast, very large. Confronted with 'descriptions of strange kinds of animals, say intermediate between man and dog, man and lion, man and hawk, etc.', the subject, who 'has seldom if ever thought of these kinds . . . and therefore never felt an urge to make up his mind to which of them to apply the predicate "Mensch"', produces a large number of ambivalent responses. The fact that the subject is thus uncertain, says Carnap, 'means that the intension of the word "Mensch" for him is not quite clear even to himself, that he does not completely understand his own word.'[16]

The thesis of universal open texture – in Carnap's language, universal intensional vagueness – implies that every term is such that the true statements in which it figures cannot be exhaustively divided into analytic and synthetic truths for any subject. Waiving anterior questions as to whether the testing procedure described is at all relevant to philosophical notions of analyticity – whether e.g. the relative and pragmatic notion it yields has epistemological significance of any sort, whether the truths labeled analytic for a given subject by the procedure can be distinguished (as meaning-dependent) from the subject's firmly held synthetic beliefs – the thesis of universal open texture holds the analytic-synthetic distinction, as above interpreted, to be always incomplete. Carnap himself holds that, while his discussion concerns 'simple pre-scientific language', the language of science continually reduces the degree of vagueness, not only of the extensional but also of the intensional variety. He also advocates, further, the laying down of explicit rules of intension to facilitate 'clear mutual understanding and effective communication.'[17]

The question to be asked relative to the latter point is whether all representations can be anticipated, and all mention-selection then freed from indecision for every term whatever. In Carnap's idiom, the question is whether all logical possibilities may be foreseen so that all intensions might be subjected to rule in advance. It may be urged that the statement of rules would, in any case, not settle the matter of open texture, since *the rules themselves* may not accurately forecast the subject's uncertainties in applying compounds to descriptions in contexts as yet unknown. A given scientific system, with stated rules of intension, might thus indeed yield decisions *relative to these rules*, but fail to anticipate the indeterminacies attending future research, occasioning revision of the very rules in question. This point is well expressed by Waismann who writes:[18]

'But are there not exact definitions at least in science?' Let's see. The notion of gold seems to be defined with absolute precision, say by the spectrum of gold with its characteristic lines. Now what would you say if a substance was discovered that looked like gold, satisfied all the chemical tests for gold, whilst it emitted a new sort of radiation? 'But such things do not happen.' Quite so; but they *might* happen, and that is enough to show that we can never exclude altogether the possibility of some unforeseen situation arising in which we shall have to modify our definition.

The deployment of compounds, as we have earlier stressed, is not routinely derivable from that of their constituents; the relevant relation earlier suggested is akin to the metaphorical extension of linguistic habits. Such a view, applied to the question of analyticity in the manner discussed above, helps perhaps to account for the temporal and cultural variability in judgments of analyticity. Taken out of the realm of logical or quasi-logical intuition and reinterpreted in terms of metaphorical, psychological, and pedagogical transfer, the traditional problem of analyticity is replaced by inquiries into the role of certain compounds in anticipating new cases and affecting their disposition by constituents, the relations of mention-selection to denotation in the course of learning, the development of representational devices satisfying various compounds etc. The thesis of universal open texture, as we have here analyzed it following interpretation (ii), is in any case an empirical thesis with great plausibility.

9 OPEN TEXTURE AND RELATIVE TERMS

We return now to the first interpretation, (i), suggested in Section 6 above. Here we deal with the term itself rather than its compounds. According to (i), the thesis of universal open texture says that there are, in fact, undecidable objects for every descriptive term; it claims, thus, that every descriptive term is vague relative to *some* domain. The weaker variant (i)' says, not that there *are* undecidable objects for every descriptive term, but only that the existence of such objects for every descriptive term is not incompatible with our present knowledge; *so far as we know*, (in other words) every descriptive term *may* be vague relative to some domain. Let us address ourselves to the less sweeping claim, since it is the more credible of the two.

Some of the appeal of this claim derives perhaps from consideration of ordinary terms and their negates, whose respective extensions (even if presumed finite) are not thought to be exhaustively known. Thus, 'horse' is not assumed to have an extension restricted to hitherto encountered instances, nor is there such a restrictive assumption for its negate, 'non-horse'. Even supposing easy decidability of all prior instances relative to this pair of terms, it is therefore not precluded that new instances of each remain which have not yet been assigned to the one or the other. We are in no position to say either that every new object must be a non-horse since all the horses have already been encountered, or that every new instance must be a horse since we have already examined all the non-horses. But then how can we be sure that remaining instances calling for fresh decisions relative to our two terms are in fact such as to lend themselves to easy decision?

It may be argued, however, that the example of such ordinary terms as e.g. 'horse' is insufficiently general to provide support for (i)'. For we can specify descriptive terms, unlike 'horse', whose extensions *are* wholly confined to (decidable) instances already encountered. Given, for example, all those things hitherto decided as falling within the extension of 'chair', we devise a new term, say '*K*-chair', understood as applying to these and only these things: Here, unlike the case of 'horse', we are indeed in a position to say that every new element must be a non-*K*-chair, all the *K*-chairs having already been exhausted.

Still, this contrast between 'horse' and '*K*-chair' rests on the common assumption that new objects are recognizable as such. Judged new, an object is decidable as a non-*K*-chair: given our capacity to recognize the novelty of instances, '*K*-chair' is indeed decidable for every domain, and the thesis of universal open texture fails. But the capacity in question can hardly be taken for granted. For all we know or can reasonably assume, there may be chairs we are unable to decide as new or old instances; for them, even '*K*-chair' is vague. The thesis (i)' thus survives after all.

The replacement of classificatory with comparative or quantitative terms has been suggested as a way of eliminating vagueness. Such replacement in science has been held to provide more flexible descriptive schemes, less likely therefore to be plagued with borderline cases. We shall see how open texture outlasts the replacement in question.

The notion that vague categorical terms may have non-vague relational counterparts is suggested by A. Church, for example, who writes as follows:[19]

> The term *relative* is applied especially to words which have been or might be thought to denote monadic propositional functions, but for some reason must be taken as denoting relations. Thus the word *short* or the notion of shortness may be called relative because as a monadic propositional function it is vague, while as a relation (*shorter than*) it is not vague.

And C. G. Hempel describes thus the idea that natural continuities are encompassed more smoothly by descriptive schemes that are comparative or quantitative than by those that are classificatory:[20]

> It has often been held that the transition from classificatory

to the more elastic comparative and quantitative concepts in science has been necessary because the objects and events in the world we live in simply do not exhibit the rigid boundary lines called for by classificatory schemata, but present instead continuous transitions from one variety to another through a series of intermediate forms. Thus, e.g., the distinctions between long and short, hot and cold, liquid and solid, living and dead, male and female, etc., all appear, upon closer consideration, to be of a more-or-less character, and thus not to determine neat classifications.

Let us now consider open texture in connection with length. Imagine a domain consisting exclusively of rods between 2 in. and 4 in. long, and rods between 10 in. and 12 in. long, to be characterized by means of the predicates 'short' and 'long'. Such a task, we suppose, presents no difficulty, rods of the first variety being described as short, those of the second variety as long. Indecision is, however, likely to set in with addition to the initial domain of rods of intermediate length; the existence of intermediate instances is, moreover, compatible with available knowledge. Even if we are given exactly two rods a and b, just noticeably different from one another in length, we cannot normally rule out the existence of a third rod c that is not noticeably different from either a or b and hence must be conceived as intermediate. Thus, if we have drawn the boundary between 'short' and 'long' precisely through the narrow separation of a from b, we still confront the open texture of these terms in the 'possible' existence of intermediate c.

Now Church, as we have seen, holds that replacement of the categorical 'short' by the relative 'shorter than' eliminates vagueness. Such elimination may indeed occur for given domains. Reverting to the example just considered, suppose that, rather than taking a as categorically short and b as categorically long, we describe a as shorter than b. Now c, not noticeably different in length from either a or b, is assigned an intermediate position and thus judged *longer than a* and *shorter than b*. Whereas c was undecidable relative to the categorical 'short' and 'long', it proves thus decidable for the relative 'shorter than' and 'longer than'. The fact that the existence of c is not incompatible with available knowledge does not therefore constitute an indication of open texture for the relative terms in question. Similarly, the indecision occasioned, in our previous example, by rods of intermediate length may be dissipated or considerably reduced in certain domains when the task of assigning categorical labels ('short', 'long') to individual rods is replaced by that of applying their relative counterparts ('shorter than', 'longer than') to pairs of rods. And, clearly, the fact that the existence of decidable pairs of intermediate rods cannot be ruled out in advance is no indication of open texture. But what guarantees that *all* intermediate pairs will be thus decidable? Granted that, for many domains where a dichotomous division of graduated elements is practically impossible, it is easy to decide each available pair relative to a suitable two-place predicate, how can we rule out the existence of pairs *undecidable* by such a predicate? In short, how can open texture be precluded?

Open texture seems, in fact, rather to be embodied in our general understandings. Applications of 'shorter than', for example, are made at any given time only down to a certain level of precision. We can, say, tell that one shelf is shorter than another if it is shorter by one half-inch or more; beneath the one half-inch level, our eye fails to distinguish. But we typically do not take such indistinguishability as incompatible with an actual difference in length; we suppose, rather, that if there is such a difference, it is inaccessible to us by our current procedure, i.e. inspection by the naked eye. In short, the case is deemed undecidable. Assuming limits to our discriminatory capacities at any given time, we are always prepared for the existence of indiscriminable but unequal pairs, allowing, to be sure, that further distinctions may eventually be made, below the level of current procedure. In sum, we presume open texture.

10 OPEN TEXTURE AND CLASSIFICATION

Analogous considerations apply also to the specification of precise logical or numerical criteria for *classification*, covering hitherto undecided cases. Such specification at best eliminates vagueness for certain choices of domain; it does not remove open texture. This point, typically overlooked, is brought out sharply by emphasis on the relativity of vagueness to domain. We consider here two examples. First, Church writes:[21]

> *longevity* is vague because, although a man who dies at sixty certainly does not possess the characteristic of longevity and one who lives to be ninety certainly does, there is doubt about a man who dies at seventy-five. On the other hand, *octogenarian* is not vague, because the precise moment at which a man becomes an octogenarian may (at least in principle) be determined.

For our second example, we consider remarks by Hempel directly following the passage quoted in the last Section. That passage outlined the view that pervasive natural continuities (e.g. between long and short, hot and cold, etc.) motivate the transition from classificatory to comparative and quantitative notions in science. Commenting on this view, Hempel continues:[22]

> But this way of stating the matter is, at least, misleading. In principle, every one of the distinctions just mentioned can be dealt with in terms of classificatory schemata, simply by stipulating certain precise boundary lines. Thus, e.g., we might, by definitional fiat, qualify the interval between two points as long or short according as, when put alongside some arbitrarily chosen standard, the given interval does or does not extend beyond the latter. This criterion determines a dichotomous division of intervals according to length. And by means of several different standard intervals, we may exhaustively divide all intervals into any not too large finite number of 'length classes', each of them having clearly specified boundaries.

In both Church's and Hempel's examples, however, the precise specification of class boundaries may eliminate vagueness, so far as we know, only for certain domains. It does not eliminate open texture, since it cannot preclude the existence of elements whose placement relative to the class boundaries in question is undecidable by current procedure. The *application* of boundary criteria, in other words, proceeds down to a given level of precision, below which the position of elements cannot be decided, while the existence of such elements cannot be ruled out.

Thus 'the precise moment at which a man becomes an octogenarian' may provide a clear decision for certain hitherto undecidable cases, i.e. the man who dies at seventy-five. But the determination of 'the precise moment' can be made, at any given time, only above a certain level of precision and no decision is forthcoming for cases beneath the operative level. To say, as Church does, that the precise moment may (at least in principle) be determined is to say, perhaps, that there is no advance limit to the precision with which this moment may be approximated, hence no limit to the increasing precision with which the theoretical boundary criterion defined by it may be applied in practice. Yet, it remains true that the application of the criterion at any given time is restricted by a level of precision in force at that time, and that the existence of elements undecidable under such restriction is not generally precluded.

In Hempel's example, too, the stipulated definition of length classes provides, let us agree, an exhaustive (and exclusive) division of intervals within our domain. We suppose that every interval in question falls into one of these classes and that, falling into one, it falls outside every other. Nevertheless, to decide, for any given interval, that it does or does not extend beyond a given standard is a matter of application, which is restricted by the relevant level of precision in force. The existence of elements undecidable under such restriction is not ruled out; thus any elimination of vagueness effected by Hempel's proposal may, so far as we know, be limited to certain domains only, and open texture remains.

We have seen, in the cases discussed above, a reduction in the scope of vagueness, for given domains, through replacement of certain categorical by relative terms ('short' by 'shorter than'), or their replacement by precise categorical counterparts ('possesses longevity' by 'octogenarian'; 'short' by 'does not extend beyond standard S'). The reduction of vagueness effected by either form of replacement in *given* domains cannot, we have argued, rule out vagueness in *all*. Even perfect mathematical precision in newly stipulated criteria does not eliminate open texture since, as we have seen, the application of such criteria is limited by levels of precision. It follows that non-vagueness must be distinguished from precision, contrary to the suggestion of Church, and in line with our general conclusions, reached earlier.[23]

Yet open texture of course allows a reduction of vagueness through stipulation of precise criteria with smaller regions of indecision than those of their originals. In place of a broad band of undecidable elements between those clearly 'long' and those clearly 'short', we saw, in Hempel's example, a confinement of undecidables (if any) to a narrow band around the newly defined standard S, reflecting the limits of our application procedure for S.

Introduction of several length classes in place of a merely dichotomous division has a further advantage, which should be noted. In the dichotomous case, we have, let us suppose, a precise redefinition of the original 'long' and 'short' by stipulation of S as the critical criterion. (See Figure 1.) Confinement of

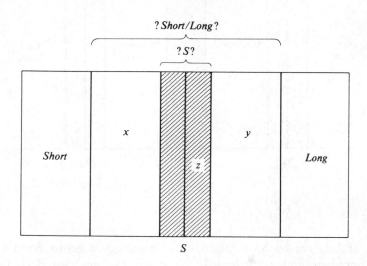

Figure 1

undecidables to the narrow hatched region ?S? may, as we have seen, reduce vagueness in certain domains, e.g. by allowing clear decision of x as short and of y as long, although they fall within the undecidable range of the original terms 'long' and 'short'. For z, however, we have no new decidability through reference to S; it was originally undecidable as long or short, and it remains so. For domains consisting wholly of elements, like z, within the region ?S?, the increased precision afforded by S yields no reduction in vagueness at all.

Suppose, now, that the original ?*Short/Long*? region is divided into several length-classes. (See Figure 2.) The vertical lines S_1,

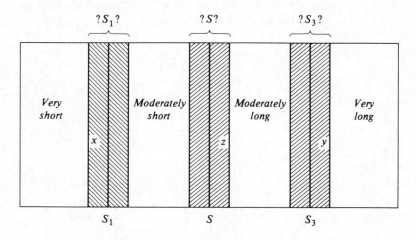

Figure 2

S, and S_3 are to be thought of as marking intervals from O, ordered by increasing length. Now any element that does not extend from O beyond S_1 (when suitably aligned) is defined as *very short*; extending beyond S_1 but not beyond S, it is *moderately short*, etc.

Considering x in *Figure 2*, we see that, although it falls within the undecidable band around S_1, it is clearly either very short or moderately short, i.e. clearly short; analogously, y is clearly long, although within the undecidable band around S_3. However, z, although (as in *Figure 1*) remaining within the undecidable region of S, is clearly decidable relative to S_1 and S_3, that is, it is clearly neither very short nor very long, hence anyhow of moderate length. The introduction of several length classes, with their respective, and non-overlapping bands of indecision, thus offers a new sort of decidability for z. The undecidability of z with respect to S does not prevent the clear exclusion of z from certain portions of the domain, for it affects only immediately adjacent regions. The persistence of open texture, for each precisely defined standard S, is thus compatible with increased specificity of placement as well as reduction of vagueness.

II VAGUENESS AND LOGIC

We have so far been construing vagueness pragmatically, as having to do with a subject's indecision in applying a term to elements of some domain. We have not, in particular, identified the *subject's difficulty* in application with the *inapplicability* (i.e. referential indeterminacy) of the term itself. Such an identification would be serious, for it would amount to a denial of the law of excluded middle, for which every object is such that every (categorially suitable) term applies to it or does not. Denial of this law, coupled with the usual understanding of negation, leads moreover to contradiction; that a is neither P nor not P implies '$\sim Pa$' and '$\sim \sim Pa$' – hence (allowing the inference from the latter to 'Pa') both '$\sim Pa$' and 'Pa'.

Whether it is *preferable* to adopt a pragmatic interpretation of vagueness or rather a semantic interpretation (along with suitable revisions of logic to avoid the contradiction noted) is a question to be faced only if we hold that a pragmatic option is genuinely available. M. Black suggests, however, that the pragmatic construal provides no independent alternative – leading inevitably to the same end as the semantic version.[24] As we have noted earlier, Black holds that all terms 'whose application involves the use of the senses' are vague. That is to say, they have *borderline cases* or *doubtful objects* 'to which we are unable to say either that the class name does or does not apply.' But to suppose that there is such a region of 'doubtful application', he argues, is itself inconsistent with conventional logic.[25] Let us consider his argument, taking 'doubtful application' to mean 'pragmatically doubtful application' – an inability of the subject to say either that the class name does or does not apply. (On the alternative semantic reading of this phrase, the whole argument is unnecessary, since the inconsistency to be demonstrated follows directly, as shown in the last paragraph.)

Black takes 'L' as a vague symbol and S as a series that is 'linear and composed of a finite number, ten say, of terms x', letting the 'rank of each term in the series be used as its name (so that the constant values of the variable x are the integers one to ten inclusive)'. Finally, he supposes the region of 'doubtful application' to 'consist of the terms whose numbers are five and six respectively'. He then argues as follows:[26]

Suppose now that L_1, L_2, L_3, L_4, are true, while L_5 and L_6 are 'doubtful'. It can only follow that to assert Lx of any x is positively to exclude it only from the range 7 to 10, since we cannot be sure, when Lx is asserted, that x does not perhaps occur in the range 5, 6. Thus to assert Lx is tantamount to confining x to the range 1 to 6.

Having obtained this result, it is easy to construct a similar argument in respect of $\sim Lx$. The assertion of $\sim Lx$ can, no more than the assertion of Lx, positively exclude x from the fringe 5, 6. It follows that to assert $\sim Lx$ is tantamount to excluding x from the range 1 to 4 and confining it to the range 5 to 10.

In short, inability to find a logical interpretation of doubtful assertions in terms of the two truth values, truth and falsehood, forces us to admit that the ranges of application of Lx, 1 to 6, and of $\sim Lx$, 5 to 10, overlap in the fringe, 5, 6.

On the other hand, the statement $\sim Lx$ is, by definition of the logical operation of negation, true only when Lx is false, and false only when Lx is true. If, as we have assumed, asserting Lx confines x to the range 1 to 6, Lx is false only when x belongs to the range of 7 to 10. Thus in contradiction to our previous result that $\sim Lx$ is true when and only when x belongs to the range 5 to 10, $\sim Lx$ should be true when and only when x belongs to the range 7 to 10. The formal properties of logical negation are incompatible with an interpretation which allows the domain and the complementary domain of a propositional function to overlap.

That the argument begins with an assumption of *pragmatically*, rather than *semantically*, doubtful objects may be seen from the fact that the first quoted paragraph supposes that 'L_5' and 'L_6' are doubtful and then concludes that 5 and 6 may nevertheless satisfy 'L', so far as we know. Were 5 and 6 supposed semantically doubtful relative to 'L', they would be held not to satisfy 'L' in any case, and the attribution of 'L' to x would positively exclude x from 5 and 6, as well as 7 to 10. Moreover, the determination that x is excluded only from 7 to 10 by reference to what we can or cannot be sure of in the act of assertion seems further evidence of a pragmatic interpretation. Thus the argument apparently purports to show that the assumption of pragmatically doubtful objects leads to logical inconsistency no less than the assumption of semantically doubtful objects.

The argument seems, however, to be mistaken, resting on a misuse of the notions of 'exclusion' and 'confinement'. In the first quoted paragraph, it is said that 'to assert Lx of any x is positively to exclude it' only from 7 to 10 since we cannot be sure x does not perhaps occur in 5, 6; hence 'to assert Lx is tantamount to confining x to the range 1 to 6.' But positive exclusion from 7 to 10 does not imply positive attribution of 'L' to the range 1 to 6: It does not imply that if x occurs anywhere within the latter range, x satisfies 'L'. By hypothesis, we cannot be sure x does not occur in 5, 6; it does not follow that if x occurs in 5, 6, then 'Lx' is true.

Nor does the *confining* of x to 1–6 imply more than that x is to be located somewhere within this range; in particular, it does not imply that any x within this range is such that Lx. If x satisfies 'L', then we may be sure it is located within 1–6; it does not follow that if it is so located then we may be sure it satisfies 'L'.

But then the contradiction to be shown fails to emerge. In the final paragraph of the quoted passage, Black says, 'If, as we have assumed, asserting Lx confines x to the range 1 to 6, Lx is false only when x belongs to the range of 7 to 10.' To say that 'Lx' confines x to the range 1 to 6 is perfectly compatible with the falsehood of 'Lx' for some x belonging to the same range. Thus, while it is acceptable to say that 'Lx' is false when x belongs to 7–10, it is not correct to say (with Black) that 'Lx' is false '*only when*' x belongs to 7–10.

In the second quoted paragraph, Black argues that to assert '$\sim Lx$' confines x to 5–10. Then, in the final quoted paragraph, he refers to this point as 'our previous result that $\sim Lx$ is true when and only when x belongs to the range 5 to 10.' But the latter description is surely unwarranted. That the assertion of '$\sim Lx$' confines x to 5–10 means that if x is not L, then it occurs within the range 5–10; it does not also mean that if x is located anywhere within the latter range, then it is not L. The phrase 'when and only when' in the above description is, in other words, too strong: 'only when' is all right, but not the initial 'when'.

The contradiction that Black claims to derive in the final quoted paragraph consists in the conjunction of the following two sentences:

(1) '$\sim Lx$' is true when and only when x belongs to 7–10.

(2) '$\sim Lx$' is true when and only when x belongs to 5–10.

As we have seen, however, 'only when' is not warranted in (1), and 'when' is not warranted in (2). In place of these two sentences, we should then properly have:

(1') '$\sim Lx$' is true when x belongs to 7–10.
(2') '$\sim Lx$' is true only when x belongs to 5–10.

These latter two sentences, (1') and (2'), are easily seen to be compatible.

Indeed, a pragmatic interpretation of this situation is directly available. If, by hypothesis, '$L5$' and '$L6$' are doubtful, then when I assert '$\sim Lx$', I am definite in my exclusion of x from 1–4 and therefore sure in locating x within 5–10. If, in asserting 'Lx', I am sure in locating x within 1–6, I am equally sure that if x occurs in 7–10, it will be true that $\sim Lx$. But there is no contradiction here. Analogously, since '$L5$' and '$L6$' are doubtful, then when I assert 'Lx', I am definite in excluding x from 7–10, and sure in locating it within 1–6. And if, in asserting '$\sim Lx$', I am sure in locating x within 5–10, I am equally sure that if x occurs in 1–4, it will be true that Lx. Again, no contradiction arises. My exclusions, confinements and feelings of doubtfulness and assurance are all consistently describable without violence to logic. The argument that a pragmatic interpretation of vagueness leads to conflict with standard logic fails.

It is, moreover, not clear that Black's own remedy really is a revision of standard logic, as he suggests. He describes this remedy as:[27]

> the introduction of more complex symbolism, replacing the propositional function Lx of a single variable by a function of two variables, $L(x, c)$ (read: 'L applies to x with consistency c'). The relations between symbols in a calculus whose symbols are assumed to be 'absolutely precise' will then appear as a limiting case of the relations between symbols having an extra argument, c, and obtained from the general case by allowing c to tend either to zero or to infinity in every formula in which it occurs, i.e., in effect simply by suppressing that argument. Thus the validity and usefulness of the relations applicable to the limiting case (logical relations between 'absolutely precise' symbols) will depend upon the degree to which they can be represented as a standard to which the more general case approximates.

But can the proposal be viewed merely as a reconstrual of 'L' as a two-place rather than a one-place predicate? The reading 'L applies to x with consistency c' is faulty for, though purporting to mention the expression 'L', it uses the expression itself rather than a name of it. Speaking about 'L', the reading properly belongs to a metalanguage of the original 'Lx'. It should, for the sake of clarity, be symbolized not as '$L(x, c)$', but rather as '$A("L", x, c)$', with the semantic three-place predicate of the metalanguage, 'A' (for 'Applies') made explicit. There is, in such symbolism, no remaining temptation to construe the metalinguistic schema as a generalization of the object language schema, 'Lx'.

Nor is there any obvious plausibility to the suggestion that the metalinguistic open sentence is a *replacement* for the object language original. The point of the former is to describe object uses of 'Lx', to refer, as Black puts it, 'to situations in which a user of the language makes a decision whether to apply L or $\sim L$ to an object x. . . . Let us call such a situation a *discrimination of x with respect to L*, or a DxL for short.'[28] Describing, in our metalanguage, the consistency of object uses of 'Lx' in DxL, we do not propose to supplant these object uses with our metalinguistic '$A("L", x, c)$'. As Black himself remarks:[29]

To remove a possible source of misunderstanding it may be as well to add that the analysis of Lx in the manner suggested does not involve the claim that a person asserting Lx in a DxL should know the analysis, i.e., the corresponding distribution of consistencies of application, either at that or at any subsequent time. Any assumption that ability to use a symbol correctly involves extensive statistical knowledge of the behavior of other users would involve a vicious circle.

To have all users of 'Lx' give it up in favor of '$A("L", x, c)$' would make the latter vacuous by removing its object. To propose that users of 'Lx' are rather to reform its employment, restricting its scope to cases where c is sufficiently high, is to invite precisely the vicious circle referred to in the passage just quoted.

If the semantic predicate 'A' does not, then, supplant the object language predicate 'L' (whose users, however naively, apparently assume the standard logic), does it, at least for the metalanguage, accomplish the wanted revision of logic in response to the phenomena of vagueness? It does not appear so, since it remains true in the metalanguage that for every term T, every object x, and every number c, T applies to x with consistency c, or T does not apply to x with consistency c. (Black defines the consistency of application of 'L' to x as the limit of the ratio m/n, where m is the number of decisions of users to apply 'L' to x while n is the number of their decisions to apply '$\sim L$' to x, when the number of users of 'L' and of DxL increase indefinitely.)

Hempel compares Black's introduction of '$L(x, c)$' to that of metrical notions generally, e.g. 'the temperature of x in centigrades is t'. He suggests 'it amounts to determining the gradations of a certain property by reference to the judgment of a sufficiently great number of experts'; allowing the procedure to be clear, Hempel argues it to be less useful scientifically than one introducing gradable concepts 'by means of more objective criteria.'[30] Now the notion that the *theorist* might, for his own special purposes, reject the object language predicate 'green', in favor of 'called "green" by such-and-such naive users with consistency c' is indeed free of our earlier objections on the score of vacuity or circularity. But it is far from evident that such a theoretical choice is wise. Although there is no general rule determining the matter, Hempel's caution as to relative objectivity needs to be taken into account, and the onus of proof is on advocates of such choice to show its desirability in any given case.

But, as Hempel notes, the adoption of '$L(x, c)$' does not, in any event,[31]

> involve any modification of the principles of logic; thus, for example, it remains true that either the temperature of x is t, or the temperature of x is not t; and analogously, Mr. Black certainly wants to maintain the principle of excluded middle with respect to expressions such as '$L(x, c)$'.

Commenting on this remark of Hempel's, Black concedes that his new terminology for vagueness 'need not' involve any modification of standard logic, but he affirms that 'we can also accept more generalized principles of inference in relation to which our present logical principles will appear to be special cases.'[32] I conclude that Black has shown neither that a pragmatic interpretation of vagueness leads to conflict with standard logic, nor that his own conceptual remedy requires any revision of such logic.

It is, of course, true that we can adopt a revised logic, but the question is whether we are required to do so, or whether it is at least clearly desirable to do so. Arguments for revisions of standard logic have been various, not all of them, by any means, based on considerations of vagueness. Rejection of the true-false division has, for example, been proposed as a remedy for paradoxes of set theory and semantics. Consider Russell's class of all classes that are not members of themselves: Is this class a member of itself or not? If not, then it is, and if it is, then it is not. 'The proposal', as Quine writes, 'is that we allow this and similar sentences the middle truth value. The equivalence, once so vexatious, of these sentences to their own negations, can thereupon be received with equanimity – negation now being, of course, the reformed negation of three-valued logic'.[33] (Negation being here construed as transforming sentences with intermediate truth values into others with intermediate truth values, the paradox evaporates.) The remedy has, in this case, however, seemed to many to be more drastic than required by the disease. As Quine has commented:[34]

the plan is not to my liking. It runs counter to a generally sound strategy which I call the maxim of minimum mutilation. The classical logic of truth functions and quantification is free of paradox, and incidentally it is a paragon of clarity, elegance, and efficiency. The paradoxes emerge only with set theory and semantics. Let us then try to resolve them within set theory and semantics, and not lay fairer fields waste.

Revisions of logic have been suggested, further, to accommodate more tightly the theoretically admissible questions of quantum mechanics, or the proper issues allowable under some variety of constructivist intuition in mathematics. The desirability of such revisions is a matter of judgment which may well be left undecided from the point of view of the present discussion – it being understood, in any case, that revisions advantageous in paring unanswerable questions from the body of science may require complications and interpretive opacities to be reckoned as significant costs. The main question to which we need to address ourselves here is this: Does the typical phenomenon of vagueness, as we have earlier discussed it, require, or even render it desirable, that classical two-valued logic be surrendered in favor of one or another revision?

12 VAGUENESS, MEANING AND FACT

The impulse to say yes is akin to the motivations just mentioned in the case of quantum theory and constructivism; the point is to eliminate from our language the capacity to frame questions deemed inadmissible. And the elimination is to be accomplished by building the incapacity into the logical structure itself. Now in the case of quantum theory and of constructivism, I have conceded the issue to be a matter of judgment, while cautioning that promised advantages need to be weighed against various costs. But the corresponding proposal to build the incapacities of vagueness into logic is in a much worse position. For whereas there are reasonably clear ways of specifying the allegedly inadmissible questions in quantum theory and in varieties of constructivism, the same cannot be said of vagueness as it has been standardly treated. Indeed, the very definitions of vagueness

72

typically offered depend on one or another variant of a distinction between meaning and fact which cannot be upheld.

Peirce's account, for example, hinges on a contrast between ignorance and the indeterminacy of linguistic habits:[35]

> A proposition is vague when there are possible states of things concerning which it is *intrinsically uncertain* whether, had they been contemplated by the speaker, he would have regarded them as excluded or allowed by the proposition. By intrinsically uncertain we mean not uncertain in consequence of any ignorance of the interpreter, but because the speaker's habits of language were indeterminate.

The question is whether this critical distinction can be made clear, whether we can distinguish an indecision attributable to ignorance of fact from one attributable to indeterminacy of habit. Habits, after all, are not formed in a vacuum; they are themselves intimately connected with states of belief, knowledge and ignorance. And general doubts concerning the analytic-synthetic distinction are inevitably aroused by what looks suspiciously like an effort to separate 'synthetic' from 'analytic' uncertainties.

Black describes a symbol's vagueness as consisting in 'the existence of objects concerning which it is intrinsically impossible to say either that the symbol in question does, or does not, apply',[36] thus replacing Peirce's 'intrinsic uncertainty' with 'intrinsic impossibility', without saying, however, how to distinguish the latter from mere (non-intrinsic, or perhaps factual?) impossibility. In another place, he appeals to language rules, taking a term to be vague if it has borderline cases, that is:[37]

> cases for which the rules of the language containing the term do not specify either that the term shall or that it shall not apply. Thus certain shades of reddish-orange in the spectrum are borderline cases for the application of the term 'red'. And 'red' is vague in the English language.

Here the account rests on a putative distinction between gaps in the linguistic *rules* governing a particular term, and gaps in our *knowledge* as to whether the conditions laid down by these rules have been satisfied in a given instance. The notion of *the* rules of a natural language is, however, too obscure to ground the distinction. To formulate the desired contrast of meaning and fact as a distinction between rules and fact is no advance.

A recent discussion by S. Haack introduces the notion of information. She describes one form of vagueness as follows:[38]

> The qualifications [for being F] are simple ... but in certain cases it is *indeterminate whether the condition, or one of the conditions, is satisfied* .... it is necessary to add, that the indeterminacy about whether the qualifications are satisfied should not be due to any lack of information about the object in question.

Lack of information is, according to Haack, to be contrasted with the lack of precise qualifications. But how is *this* contrast to be made? Would not such qualifications, were they supplied, count as adding information about the object in question? Or is the point rather to distinguish merely factual or contingent items of information from those that formulate qualifications and thus are to be taken as expressing necessary truths? Perhaps the latter idea underlies Haack's explanation: 'By "the qualifications for being F" is understood: the filling of a true sentence-scheme of the form "Necessarily $(x$ is F iff . . .)"'.[39] If so, the fundamental contrast required hinges rather on necessity than on information, and provides no advantage over earlier suspect talk of 'intrinsic impossibility'.

A final illustration involves the notion of *evidence*. W. P. Alston writes:[40]

> A term is said to be vague if there are cases in which there is no definite answer as to whether the term applies. 'Middle-aged' is vague in this sense. ... There seem to be bands on either side of the clear cases of middle age where it is not clear what we should say. To say that there *is* no definite answer is not to say that we have not yet been able to give a definite answer because of insufficient evidence. The preceding point about 'middle-aged' is to be sharply distinguished from the fact that we are not able to say whether the term 'inhabited planet' is to be applied to Mars. In this case, we know reasonably well what kind of observations would lead to a positive or negative answer; it is just that, at present, we are not in a position to make those observations. But when we are unable to say whether

a 41-year-old man is middle-aged, it is not because we have
not yet made certain observations that would settle the
question. It is not as if we could decide this point by settling
certain questions about the average blood pressure or
metabolic rate of 41-year-old men. We have no idea what
would definitely settle the question. It is not that we have not
succeeded in finding the answer; there is no answer. This
shows that the situation is due to an aspect of the meaning of
the term, rather than to the current state of our knowledge.

Alston wants to distinguish cases in which there *is* no answer
from cases in which we have been unable to find the answer
because of insufficient evidence, knowing full well, however,
what sorts of observations would constitute sufficient evidence.
What he overlooks is the role of theory in defining criteria of
evidential relevance.

In advance of adequate theory, we may be unable to say what
would constitute sufficient evidence for applying a given term;
the emergence of an adequate theory may make clear for the first
time the relevance of various observations as evidence for such
application. The subtle tests required to decide whether there is
any form of life on Mars depend, in fact, upon a wide variety of
theoretical assumptions. In advance of our having acquired the
relevant theory, would it have been proper to say: 'There *is* no
answer to the question of life on Mars; this is a matter of the
meaning of terms rather than the current state of our knowledge'?

Alston considers just two cases, one in which we have sufficient
theory to define relevant evidence, and another where we have
no criteria of relevant evidence – identifying the latter as a case
involving meaning, hence a case in which there *is* no answer to
be sought. What he misses is a third case, in which we have no
evidential criteria because we have as yet no adequate theory,
this being a matter of the state of our current knowledge. From
the fact that 'We have no idea what would definitely settle the
question', he concludes, 'It is not that we have not succeeded in
finding the answer; there is no answer'.[41] If, however, we must
indeed reckon with the prospect that in certain cases a theory to
be found will furnish an answer later on, then a critical distinction
must still be provided to separate such cases, where our present
theory is inadequate, from those other presumed cases where our

meanings are indeterminate. But *this* distinction is not provided in the discussion we have been considering.

It might be thought that a distinction is to be found in the way the operative indecision in a term's application may be remedied. In the one case, a theory is to be supplied; in the other, a definition. By now, it should, however, be recognized that the contrast between statements as theories and statements as definitions is itself suspect, as is the related contrast between factual discovery and definitional legislation. To construct a fruitful definition is to have made a discovery; to find a theory is to propose it, to legislate it and test it by its consequences. In these remarks, I am following the well-known emphasis of Quine in several of his writings. For example, he concludes his paper 'On Carnap's Views on Ontology' with these words:[42]

> Science is a unified structure, and in principle it is the structure as a whole, and not its component statements one by one, that experience confirms or shows to be imperfect. Carnap maintains that ontological questions, and likewise questions of logical or mathematical principle, are questions not of fact but of choosing a convenient conceptual scheme or framework for science; and with this I agree only if the same be conceded for every scientific hypothesis.

Abandoning the analytic-synthetic distinction as well as the contrast between statements chosen and statements registering findings of fact, one cannot readily make sense of vagueness as indecision based on meaning deficiency rather than factual ignorance. It is thus somewhat disconcerting to consider Quine's discussion of vagueness in *Word and Object*. True, he does not reintroduce the suspect distinctions earlier expunged from his philosophy, and his interest is largely in connecting vagueness with language learning. Still, he adopts some of the conventional terminology of other treatments that do distinguish meaning from fact, e.g. he speaks of 'the penumbral objects of a vague term', remarking that:[43]

> the learning process being an implicit induction on the subject's part regarding society's usage, the penumbral cases are the cases for which that induction is most inconclusive for want of evidence. The evidence is not there to be gathered, society's

members having themselves had to accept similarly fuzzy edges
when they were learning. Such is the inevitability of vagueness
on the part of terms learned in the primitive way; and it tends
to carry over to other terms defined on the basis of these.

One wants, in any case, to suppose that Quine is not putting too
much weight on the word 'usage' in the first sentence (as a
surrogate for 'meanings') and that the social fuzziness he describes
may be thought of as shared ignorance rather than, or indistinguishable from, meaning indeterminacy.

Perhaps this reading is borne out by the fact that in the later
Philosophy of Logic, when Quine lists the reasons offered for
deviation from classical logic, he does not cite vagueness at all.
Moreover, he does mention 'a confusion between knowledge
and truth', stating:[44]

> Certainly there is a vast intermediate domain of sentences
> between those that we know or even believe to be true and
> those that we know or believe to be false; but we can still hold
> that each of those intermediate sentences is either true,
> unbeknownst to us, or false unbeknownst to us.

Here, indecision is clearly held not to require the postulation of
anything beyond ignorance; no further place is given to indecision based on meaning fuzziness.

To return to the main thread of argument, I have said that the
proposal to build the incapacities of vagueness into logic is in
much worse shape than analogous proposals based on positive
theoretical reasons of a physical or mathematical sort. For the
very separation of vagueness – as meaning indecision – from
ignorance of fact, cannot be upheld. Why, if this is indeed the
case, should logical import be ascribed to certain indecisions as
contrasted with others? And why select certain forms of ignorance
for enshrinement in logic rather than holding logic compatible
with any kind or degree of reduction of ignorance with the
advance of inquiry?

The notion of vagueness as purely semantic indecision seems
to me misguided. Instances of indecision do not originate either
wholly in deficiencies of meaning or wholly in deficiencies of
fact; the very distinction here presupposed is itself philosophically deficient. Surrendering it, we remain, at each moment,

with a whole variety of indecisions that vary subtly with the circumstances within which occasions for decision arise. The process of advancing inquiry often resolves such indecisions, and none should be prejudged as impervious to further investigation and resolution. Here is positive reason for holding fast to classical logic as a framework capable of accommodating, without structural alteration, any type or degree of reduction of indecision, any elimination of ignorance. Absolute vagueness evaporates as a special category, to be replaced by a contextual counterpart signifying, in each case, a particular indecision theoretically soluble by further inquiry.

III

METAPHOR

We have twice had occasion, in earlier discussions, to touch briefly on the topic of metaphor. First, having introduced the notion of elementary ambiguity, we remarked that such ambiguity comprehends metaphor, a metaphorical predicate-inscription within D characterizable as having a divergent replica therein, offering some clue to the application of the former.[1]

Secondly, in introducing the notion of mention-selection, we suggested that denotative and mention-selective uses are intimately connected in the learning process, exhibiting transfer phenomena reminiscent of metaphor: No picture *is* a man; yet, forced onto a given array of pictures, a 'man' inscription will not function arbitrarily, but will select man-pictures in fact.[2] Such selection is of course not innate, guided as it is by prevailing styles of picturing. In turn, every selection strengthens, refines, or elaborates prevalent representational standards, helping to embed each sign within a recognizable family of signs.

In suggesting that mention-selection is reminiscent of metaphor, I do not mean to imply that it can be taken as a typical case of metaphorical transfer. A salient point of resemblance is the fact that, in both cases, terms may be employed in ways felt to be not only precluded but apt. Nevertheless, there is also a critical difference which requires notice. Mention-selection does not fade under prolonged repetition: To caption a man-picture 'man' is an act that does not lose its mention-selective character even after frequent analogous mention-selections. Metaphorical use, by contrast, fades into literal use; metaphors die. That is to say, metaphorical applications by given coextensive replicas give way, after a while, to literal applications by further such replicas. The metaphorical past of the latter applications may even become obscured and require considerable effort to reconstruct. Even if original literal uses have also survived, i.e. if replicas are still being employed that are coextensive with original (pre-metaphorical) inscriptions, they typically afford no practical clue to the later divergent application, and we now have simple *E*-ambiguity rather than metaphor in particular. For we have extensionally divergent replicas, all literal, in concurrent use, i.e. in a suitable *D* contained within sufficiently recent temporal bounds.

A comparison of peculiarly metaphorical with other sorts of *E*-ambiguity will now introduce the main problem of metaphor to which our further discussion will be addressed. It will be recalled that two inscriptions are *E*-ambiguous with respect to one another if and only if they are replica-related and extensionally divergent. Now these conditions are met by accidental inscription-pairs and by indicator pairs, as well as by metaphorical-literal pairs.

In the case of *accidental pairs*, knowledge of one inscription's extension gives no clue or special advantage in determining that of the other. Consider two 'cape'-inscriptions, of which one denotes certain articles of clothing and the other denotes certain land areas. To determine the extension of one of these inscriptions is of no help in determining that of the other. Repeated exposure to replicas coextensive with the first gives no added assistance in judging the denotation of replicas coextensive with the second. Now imagine three replicas, every two of which make up an accidental pair (e.g. three 'case'-inscriptions, one denoting examples of a certain sort, one applying to legal actions, and the third denoting cartons containing bottles of wine). Finding the extension of any two of these is of no more help in determining that of the third than finding the extension of only one. There appears to be no useful diagnostic regularity projecting from already determined instances to divergent instances yet to come.

In the case of *indicator pairs,* by contrast, extensional variation relates regularly to contextual features in a way that furnishes a useful clue to new instances. Thus, an 'I' normally denotes its own producer and a 'here' refers to a suitable spatial region within which it lies. True, the apprehension of such regularities normally requires exposure to a variety of divergent indicator replicas. Thus, knowing the extension of only one such inscription, or even of several of its coextensive replicas, may give no advantage in determining the extension of a new divergent replica. Yet, unlike the case of accidental pairs, finding the extensions of additional, divergent, replicas here gives a clear advantage in interpreting still newer instances.

The case of *metaphorical-literal* pairs seems to lie between the two sorts just considered, sharing certain features with each, but not assimilable to either. To begin with, metaphorical-literal pairs are unlike accidental pairs. For, as we have seen, knowing the extension of one member of an accidental pair gives no advantage in determining that of the other; nor does knowledge of all but the last link in a chain of accidental pairs yield any help in determining the last extension. There is no scope for ingenuity in finding this last extension; the problem resembles that of learning a new language from scratch.

In the case of metaphor, however, ingenuity clearly has a place. Knowing the extension of the literal member of the pair, one has a definite advantage in determining the extension of its metaphorical replica. Finding this extension is not like learning a new language from scratch; it is rather a matter of employing the old language in solving a new problem. Whereas, moreover, ambiguities of accidental sort may usefully be encompassed in dictionary entries, the same cannot be said of metaphorical ambiguities, which continually break new ground. Here the interpreter cannot rely on the record of past metaphors. He must rather try to understand the fresh metaphorical inscription through recourse to its literal counterpart.

Now in this respect the case of metaphor resembles that of indicators. For the understanding of indicator replicas is also not encompassed in dictionary entries but rather brings to bear the import of prior divergent replicas. Yet there is still an important difference. Among indicators, extensional variation is regularly related to contextual features. No comparable regularities are available for metaphors any more than for accidental pairs;

that is to say, no such regularities govern individual literal-metaphorical pairs and, *a fortiori*, no single regularity governs all. Learning the regularities characteristic of indicators may, indeed, call for ingenuity. Having been learned, however, such regularities generally require no special ingenuity for their application, i.e. for finding the contextual features pertinent to each inscription. Metaphor, in this respect, is strikingly different. In no case does the interpreter have a regularity that, once learned, eliminates the need for ingenuity thereafter, leaving only routine inquiry into specified contextual features. On the contrary, metaphor always poses a fresh challenge to the interpreter.

The main problem is to explain its success in communication. How is the application of a metaphorical inscription discerned if it diverges from all its prior replicas, is unanticipated by dictionary entries, and escapes capture by contextual regularities? How can the understanding of prior literal replicas offer an advantage that carries over to metaphorical replicas without the help of underlying regularities? Yet how, if the need for ingenuity is never overcome (unlike accidental pairs for which it is of no avail, and indicator pairs for which it is unnecessary), can there be such regularities guiding the interpretation of metaphorical inscriptions?

Various approaches to the interpretation of metaphor have been suggested and I shall organize my remarks by reference to six such approaches, which I call: (a) the *intuitionistic*, (b) the *emotive*, (c) the *formulaic*, (d) the *intensional*, (e) the *interactional*, and (f) the *contextual*.[3] I do not mean to suggest that these labels refer to cohesive schools of thought; they are devices for highlighting theoretical directions that I judge to have central philosophical interest.

2 INTUITIONISTIC APPROACH TO METAPHOR

For the *intuitionistic* approach, metaphorical meaning cannot be derived by formula from analysis of literal constituents; added on to these constituents, such meaning requires an act of intuition for its discernment. M. Beardsley interprets such an approach, which he calls 'the supervenience theory', as beginning with the observation that metaphor 'is capable of conveying meanings that literal language cannot convey.'[4] According to this theory, Beardsley writes, 'the meaning of a metaphor does not grow out of the literal meanings of its parts, but appears as something extraneous to, and independent of, them. The literal meanings are overridden and lost; the metaphorical meaning is inexplicable in terms of them.'[5] In this respect, metaphor is thought to be analogous to, or (as Beardsley puts it) 'a species of' idiom.[6]

Yet, while idioms proper are typically treated as independent items, to be learned as such, and indeed recorded as separate units in dictionaries, metaphors can be understood, in favorable cases, through recourse to prior literal meanings and without reliance on dictionary entries. Since, however, the meaning of a metaphor does not derive from the meanings of its parts, it is accessible, if at all, not through analysis, but through an act of intuition that bridges the gulf between the past literal applications of constituents and the emergent metaphorical application of the whole. 'A metaphor cannot be construed from the interactions of its parts; it calls for a special act of intuition.'[7]

In illustration of the view under consideration, Beardsley cites M. Foss who, he says, 'seems to hold that in a metaphorical attribution, the separate terms lose all sense of their original designations and that "the metaphorical sphere . . . realizes a simple and indivisible unity."'[8] In the metaphorical process, writes Foss, 'the known symbols in their relation to each other are only material; they undergo a complete change in losing their familiar meaning in each other and give birth to an entirely new knowledge beyond their fixed and addible multitude.'[9]

An important feature of the intuitionistic approach is its affirmation of the power of metaphor to outstrip the range of literal expression and its consequent denial that metaphors are always replaceable by literal equivalents. This denial itself, however, requires analytic attention. For what criteria of replaceability are here in point? If equivalence of, say, emotivity or suggestiveness is required, then it is no more to be expected that literal expressions will find literal replacements than that metaphorical expressions will. But then, rather than offering a contrast between analysis and intuition – the first suitable for grasping the meaning of literal expressions, the latter for grasping that of metaphorical ones – the intuitionistic approach offers us no contrast at all. For the literal paraphrase of literal expressions is no more feasible than such paraphrase of metaphorical expressions. Intuition is required everywhere.

If, alternatively, equivalence is understood as specifically cognitive in reference rather than having to do with emotivity, suggestiveness or other supposed non-cognitive features, there are still various interpretations to be considered. Does cognitive equivalence imply synonymy, for example? If so, the claim of non-replaceability is too obscure to be taken seriously, or else it is, once again, clearly true not only of metaphorical but also of literal expressions. Does equivalence require translatability? Then, since the latter notion is flexible, varying with purpose and context, it is hardly surprising to say that metaphor 'is capable of conveying meanings that literal language cannot convey',[10] i.e. that metaphor may, in certain contexts and given certain purposes, be untranslatable. For the same may indeed be truly said of literal expressions. Again, the intended contrast of analysis and intuition evaporates.

Suppose the equivalence in question is taken as co-extensiveness. The claim is then, let us suppose, that metaphors are not always replaceable by literal expressions extensionally equivalent to them and belonging to the language in question; metaphors may bring powers of expression to the language that were previously unavailable. This claim too, while true, is not peculiar to metaphorical as contrasted with literal terms. A new literal primitive term of a systematic language adds to the power of the language in question.

However, it might be argued, no one supposes that the learning of a new primitive term is guided by already available primitives, whereas the meaning of a new metaphorical expression is in fact somehow grasped through reliance on available literal counterparts. Does this not show a special role for intuition in the realm of metaphor? The contrast itself may be conceded to exist; in fact, the description of it points to the problem of metaphor with which we started. Nevertheless, this contrast is not explained by the analysis-intuition distinction invoked by the intuitionist. For learning the application of a new primitive term hardly fits any evident norm of analysis, and describing the process of understanding metaphorical expressions as an act of intuition does nothing more than put a name to the mystery.

Several obscurities of the intuitionistic approach should now be noted. For one thing, the statement of the approach with which our discussion began purports to refer to meanings as entities; for another, its denial that metaphorical meanings 'grow out of' the literal meanings of their parts is hardly clear. Perhaps the point is to deny that there is a formula which, applied to the literal constituents of any metaphorical compound expression, yields a literal formulation of its metaphorical meaning. If so, the relation of this *anti-formula* thesis to the intuitionistic *anti-replaceability* thesis we have been considering (i.e. the denial that metaphorical expressions are always replaceable by literal equivalents) needs clarification.

Suppose, to begin with, that the anti-formula thesis is true, that there is no formula or systematic method yielding the metaphorical meaning of any compound expression, given solely information concerning its literal constituents. It does not follow that there is no such formula or method operating upon a wider, or a different, informational base. Nor, *a fortiori*, does it follow that the anti-replaceability thesis is true. For even if there is no method for deriving the metaphorical meaning of an expression from specified, presumably available, information, such meaning may in fact be shared by a literal equivalent.

Now suppose the anti-replaceability thesis to be true. Does it follow that the anti-formula thesis is true? Not if the requisite relativization to language is taken into account. The anti-replaceability thesis is, after all, groundless if taken absolutely; a metaphorical expression is always replaceable by a literal equivalent in *some* language: if there is no equivalent ready to hand, one can be coined at will. The thesis gains plausibility from the consideration that metaphors often seem to add power to the *particular* languages (or sublanguages) in which they arise, i.e. that metaphorical expressions seem not replaceable by literal equivalents (or sufficiently short literal equivalents) *therein*.

Interpreted thus, however, the anti-replaceability thesis does not imply that there is *no* formula applicable to the constituents of an expression to yield its metaphorical meaning. For there may, compatibly with this thesis, indeed be such a formula specifying the relevant metaphorical meaning in literal terms *outside* the language in question. Consider a simple language L that contains as extralogical terms just the proper names 'John' and 'Robert', and the single predicate, 'is a lion'. Then the metaphorical sentence 'John is a lion' has no literal equivalent within L. A formula may, however, be imagined specifying its metaphorical meaning in literal terms falling outside L, and belonging to a suitable language L'. Such a formula might, for example, be: For any sentence S in L consisting of a proper name followed by 'is a lion', the metaphorical meaning of S in L is the same as the literal meaning of the sentence S' of L' consisting of the identical proper name (also contained in L') followed by the predicate of L', 'is brave'. Or, perhaps: For any false sentence S in L of the form '—is a . . .', its metaphorical meaning is the same as the literal meaning of S' in L', where S' is the result simply of replacing 'is' in S with the predicate of L', 'resembles'. These examples, artificial as they are, show that (contrary to the suggestion of intuitionistic formulations) the anti-replaceability thesis does not imply the anti-formula thesis.

Let us take stock: Intuitionism is correct in holding that metaphors may bring additional powers of expression to the languages in which they arise. Appeal to intuition, however, does nothing to explain how the understanding of metaphors is guided by past literal language. Since, moreover, the anti-formula thesis is independent of anti-replaceability, it is possible to agree that metaphors may add expressive power to their initial languages, while yet supposing that a formula exists capable of specifying the meanings of metaphorical expressions on the basis of information about their constituents (though not always within the bounds of their respective initial languages). This is in fact a view we shall encounter in our discussion of the formulaic approach below. (A variant upholds a weaker form of anti-replaceability, i.e. denying that metaphorical expressions are always replaceable by *sufficiently short* literal equivalents within their initial languages, but supposing that there is a suitable formula for the specification of metaphorical meaning – unconstrained, however, by length or language restrictions.)

Intuitionism, as here interpreted, stands opposed to both these possibilities. It affirms the anti-formula thesis independently, denying the existence of formulas for specifying metaphorical meanings, at whatever length, and within or without the relevant initial languages. But if indeed the anti-formula thesis does not follow from anti-replaceability, what are intuitionism's grounds for affirming it? The main point is the fact that understanding a metaphorical expression seems always to pose a new challenge to interpretive ingenuity, rather than resting on either dictionary or structural regularity. In addition, intuitionism rejects particular formulas (such as the 'resemblance' formula of our recent example) as inadequate to explain metaphor. (We shall treat the bases of such rejection in discussing the formulaic approach.)

Because intuitionism affirms the anti-formula thesis as well as anti-replaceability, it dissociates metaphor from indicator terms, guided by contextual regularities, and tends to assimilate it rather to idioms and coinages, i.e. to the accidental pairs earlier discussed. Yet intuitionism recognizes that, whereas the grasp of idioms and coinages is not guided by past usage, the understanding of metaphors is. Thus while no one is tempted to suggest that idioms or coinages are comprehended through bridging acts of intuition, the case of metaphor seems to invite such interpretation.

The appeal to intuition, however, provides no positive explanation; it simply puts a label on the problem. How is the purportedly intuitive act itself guided by prior divergent applications in understanding fresh metaphorical expressions? How can such guidance, unmediated by formula, yet inform the grasp of the novel? Intuition is here no simple leap in the dark, 'the separate terms losing all sense of their original designations.'[11] It is indeed creative and addressed to the hitherto unencountered, but it also builds upon prior understandings and past applications. Whether the process be labeled 'intuition' or not, the achievement of the understanding in coping with metaphor still requires explanation.

3 EMOTIVISM AND METAPHOR

The *emotive* approach lays stress upon the capacity of metaphors to evince or arouse feelings, as distinct from conveying information. Unlike the intuitionistic insistence on the power of metaphor to outstrip the cognitive range of literal expression, the emotive view emphasizes rather that metaphor goes beyond literal language in its capacity to affect feeling.

In its extreme form, the view is that metaphorical expressions have no cognitive content (or meaning) at all, that they serve not as referential but rather as affective devices only. In a more moderate version, the idea is that while metaphors do have cognitive content, it is their emotive content (or meaning) which is distinctive; so far as cognitive content is concerned, they are replaceable by literal equivalents, but as respects their affective features, they are not in general replaceable. In its mildest formulation, emotivism allows that metaphors may in fact add to the cognitive resources of their respective languages, but insists that it is the emotive role of such metaphors that is of primary importance: The use of metaphor is not sufficiently motivated by its cognitive increment over literal expression; the affective point is rather the key.[12]

The extreme and the middle versions of emotivism both hold metaphors to be eliminable without loss of cognitive content, the former supposing them to be simply eliminable, the latter taking them to be eliminable in favor of literal equivalents. The middle and the mild versions, on the other hand, both affirm that metaphors have cognitive content, but agree that the conveying of such content does not constitute their primary function.

The extreme and the middle versions, unlike intuitionism, uphold the *replaceability* thesis, while the mild version comes close. However, this thesis, as earlier discussed, is solely *cognitive* in import. The emotive approach, upholding (or virtually upholding) this (cognitive) replaceability thesis, denies that metaphors are ever replaceable with respect to their *emotive* content – whether within or outside of their respective home languages. As to the (cognitive) *formula* thesis discussed earlier, emotivism is non-committal, but it certainly precludes the idea of a formula for generating an account of the emotive meaning of metaphor out of information about constituents. To sum up, intuitionism, taking meaning as uniformly cognitive, affirms the distinctive reach of metaphor by stressing its cognitive irreplaceability and the resistance of its (cognitive) meaning to formula. On the other hand, the emotive approach, taking meaning to be emotive as well as cognitive, emphasizes the emotive irreplaceability of metaphor and the resistance of its emotive meaning to formula.

Now the extreme version of emotivism is the view that metaphors lack all cognitive content, functioning solely as emotive devices. It is supposed that the word combinations involved in a metaphorical attribution violate standing presumptions as to the proper relations among terms, thus signaling that normal cognitive values have become inoperative. With such values in abeyance, emotive meanings come to the fore. Beardsley provides the following illustration: (Note that his term 'meaningful' is restricted to the cognitively meaningful.)[13]

> For example, the sharpness of a knife can be tested by various means, so that the phrase 'sharp knife' is meaningful. We may also suppose that 'sharp' has some negative emotive import, deriving from our experience with sharp things. Now, when we speak of a 'sharp razor' or a 'sharp drill', the emotive import is not active, because these phrases are meaningful. But when we speak of a 'sharp wind', a 'sharp dealer', or a 'sharp tongue', the tests for sharpness cannot be applied, and therefore, though the individual words are meaningful, the combinations of them are not. In this way the emotive import of the adjective is released and intensified.

Whereas Beardsley requires of cognitively meaningful terms that they have tests of applicability, the point of his example may be put more generally in terms of the normal presumptions underlying word combinations. Thus, the word 'sharp' is cognitively meaningful in a given context only when such context is compatible with our normal presumptions, e.g. in the phrase 'sharp knife'. However, it loses its cognitive meaning in a context that violates these presumptions, e.g. when (as in 'sharp wind', etc.) 'sharp' is applied to something that does not have a thin cutting edge or a fine point. In 'sharp wind', then, the meaning of 'sharp' is purely emotive, that is, it serves to evince or evoke negative feelings and to direct them at what is referred to by 'wind'. The purely cognitive content of 'A sharp wind preceded the storm' is fully retained by 'A wind preceded the storm'; the only thing lost in going from the former sentence to the latter is the expression of negative feeling directed by the former at the wind.

This account, however, seems plainly false. Not all winds are sharp winds; to say that a sharp wind preceded the storm is to provide more information than is conveyed by saying merely that a wind preceded the storm. 'Sharp wind' has an extension and it differs from the extension of 'wind' itself; thus the elimination of 'sharp' from the phrase clearly alters the reference and, hence, the cognitive content of the containing sentence. It might in fact be true that a wind preceded the storm but false that a sharp wind preceded the storm.

That 'wind' diverges from 'sharp wind' is naturally attributable to the extension of (the metaphorical) 'sharp' within this phrase, but the latter extension differs from that of (the literal) 'sharp' within 'sharp knife'. We thus have here in fact two extensions for 'sharp' rather than simply one extension plus an emotive meaning. The extreme version of the emotive approach is thus untenable.

Consider now the more moderate version, for which metaphors do have cognitive content but are replaceable, so far as this content is concerned, by literal equivalents. What is distinctive and important about metaphor, for this view, is not its cognitive content, always otherwise expressible, but rather its emotive meaning, which in general lacks suitable equivalents. All the cognitive content of 'A sharp wind preceded the storm' is preserved after replacing 'sharp' with a literal equivalent, as in e.g. 'A very cold wind preceded the storm'. It is emotive meaning that is lost. For to prefix 'wind' with 'sharp' (rather than 'very cold') overrides a presumptive restriction on the use of this adjective, producing surprise, heightening awareness, and triggering the negative feelings associated with sharp things. 'Sharp' thus has no surplus cognitive content as compared with its literal equivalents; it has, rather, additional emotive content.

Insofar as moderate emotivism depends on the (cognitive) replaceability thesis, it is suspect. For the claim that metaphorical expressions always have literal replacements within their respective languages is no more convincing for metaphorical than it is for literal expressions. Without this claim, the moderate version merges with the mildest formulation of emotivism, conceding that metaphors may add to the cognitive powers of their respective languages, but insisting that it is their emotive function which is, in any case, of primary importance.

This claim is difficult to make out. Once distinctive cognitive effect is conceded to metaphor, how can it be said that emotive function is in every case dominant in metaphorical expression? The single expression, after all, selects what it refers to and evinces or arouses emotion directed toward it; the form and quality of the emotion are typically shaped by the object selected. Is there, nevertheless, some respect in which the (cognitive) selection is not as important as the evincing or arousal of the emotion, some respect in which the object is merely incidental? Psychologists have in fact discussed a phenomenon of displacement, in which an emotion growing out of encounter with one object, and appropriate to it, is vented by directing it at another.[14] Where such a phenomenon occurs, it might perhaps be said that the venting itself is psychologically primary and the selected object incidental. But it would certainly be extravagent to claim that every metaphorical expression is a vehicle for such emotional displacement – that 'sharp wind', for example, may not simply express negative feelings aroused by, and appropriately directed at, the wind rather than displaced from something else.

The idea that all metaphors are peculiarly emotive, in any sense, is hardly convincing. 'They can be emotive,' writes Beardsley, 'and many of them are; they don't have to be. Perhaps a sharp wind is a wind we don't particularly care for, but "sharp wind" is not highly emotive, like "birdbrain" or "stinker"'.[15] Literal terms, too, are variable in emotivity, and many of them, moreover, are highly emotive, e.g. 'hydrogen bomb', 'cancer'. Emotions, after all, develop in the most intimate connection with cognitions; feelings respond to things as apprehended and comprehended.[16] Why should literal accounts of things be any less related to the emotive life than metaphorical accounts? Why should emotional response to things cognized be better expressed by metaphorical than literal reference to such things?

There is, in any case, no consensus on application of the phrase 'emotive meaning' nor does any likely empirical interpretation sustain the philosophical weight it has been made to bear. Emotive approaches to ethics, aesthetics, and metaphysics, as well as metaphor, have sought a sharp distinction between one or another of these spheres (on the one hand) and the realm of science, cognition, or literal description (on the other).[17] In no case, however, has an adequate distinction been drawn on the basis of emotivity, under a clear and independent empirical interpretation. To be sure, various plausible distinctions may be proposed between emotive and cognitive features themselves. Independent argument is required, however, if any such distinction is claimed to underly the division of forms of thought or types of expression. We have already seen the weakness of such argument with respect to the literal and the metaphorical. I conclude that moderate and mild versions of the emotive approach are also untenable.

4 FORMULAIC APPROACH TO METAPHOR

The *formulaic* approach supposes that there is some formula (or manageable set of formulas) which, given available information about literal constituents, specifies in literal terms the meanings of metaphorical expressions (though not always within the bounds of their respective initial languages). This approach, as we have seen, is compatible with anti-replaceability; it cannot be defeated simply by refuting the thesis of replaceability. Nor can it be demonstrated by establishing replaceability. Intuitionism, however, brings independent considerations to bear against it.

The basic point, noted above, is the apparent ineliminability of ingenuity in treating metaphorical expressions. The understanding of such an expression, for intuitionism, always poses a challenge beyond the reach of structural regularity and beyond the capacity of dictionaries to resolve. This sort of consideration, urged by intuitionism, seems substantial. How, despite it, does the formulaic approach hope to press its claims?

First of all, it rejects any suggestion that intuition affords an explanation of metaphorical understanding. If such understanding is to be made intelligible, we must do more than invoke special mental acts postulated to serve as its vehicles; the process or mechanism of the understanding must be made plain. This process is one that, after all, employs information about past cases to determine new applications. Despite all appearances to the contrary, then, it must be guided by rules or principles capable of making the transition.

Secondly, the formulaic approach points to familiar principles that cover at least some cases of transferred application, e.g. *synecdoche*, in which (roughly speaking) past literal application and new application stand in a part-whole or a genus-species relation. Where such principles fail to yield an interpretation, a special principle, characteristic of metaphor, comes to the fore, i.e. one resting on resemblance, similarity or iconicity. And this principle both guides interpretation and requires ingenuity. For, in making explicit the bases of resemblance left tacit by a given metaphorical expression, the interpreter cannot operate by routine. Possible similarities need to be searched, appropriate ones determined and the rest rejected. The formulaic approach thus relates metaphor intimately to simile.

The notion of metaphor as implicit simile is indeed the prevalent general view, and the idea of comparison as the underlying process of metaphorical understanding is its chief corollary. Whately put it thus: 'The Simile or Comparison may be considered as differing in form only from a Metaphor; the resemblance being in that case *stated*, which in the Metaphor is implied.'[18] A recent account by Alston relates similarity, as the principle underlying metaphor, to principles underlying figurative uses of other sorts. Having explained the figurative use of an expression as such use of the expression as diverges from all its established senses but is nevertheless intelligible 'to a fairly sensitive person with a command of the language', Alston continues:[19]

It is obvious that this sort of thing is possible only if these uses are somehow derivative from uses in established senses. Otherwise a knowledge of the standard senses would do nothing to enable a listener, however sensitive, to see what is being said. We can distinguish different kinds of figurative use in terms of the basis of derivation. Where the derivation is on the basis of a part-whole relationship, as when we say, 'The first ship opened fire' (it is a part of the ship that literally opened fire) or a genus-species relationship, as 'I have not spoken to a single creature for a week' (that is, I have spoken to no men, a species of creature), one traditionally speaks of *synecdoche*. The term 'metonymy' has been used to cover cases in which the transfer is made on the basis of any one of a number of relationships, such as cause-effect, as when we say of a performer, 'He got a good hand' (that is, he got a lot of something produced by hands) or container-contained, as in 'The White House had no comment.' (None of these are figurative uses, as I have just defined that notion, because in all these cases the expressions in question are being used in established senses. These are examples of figurative *senses*. But they can serve as examples of kinds of basis of derivation.)

Metaphor is that sort of figurative use in which the extension is on the basis of similarity.

Without mastery of the established sense of a term, one cannot hope to comprehend its metaphorical use, yet such use is not a use of the term *in an established sense*. 'One is,' as Alston puts it, 'somehow using the term to say something different, though related, and working *through* the established sense in order to do this.'[20] Giving a more detailed account of the 'mechanics of the operation',[21] Alston calls upon the work of Henle which appeals to the notion of iconicity – the expression in question serving, through an established (or literal) sense, to specify what is to be taken as an icon of the thing referred to metaphorically. In Henle's words:[22]

Metaphor, then, is analyzable into a double sort of semantic relationship. First, using symbols in Peirce's sense, directions are given for finding an object or situation. This use of language is quite ordinary. Second, it is implied that any object or situation fitting the direction may serve as an icon of what one wishes to describe. The icon is never actually present; rather, through the rule, one understands what it must be and, through this understanding, what it signifies.

Taking as an example the words of Shakespeare's Macbeth,

Sleep that knits up the ravell'd sleave of care,

(Act II, scene ii)

Alston (following Henle) considers the line to be doing two things: (a) specifying a person knitting up a ravelled cloth sleeve and (b) offering the action as an icon of the effect of sleep on someone with cares. A metaphorical expression works in this way, says Alston, only if 'there *is* some important and readily noticeable similarity between the two situations; such similarity is a necessary condition of successful metaphor.'[23] Nevertheless, metaphor is not therefore indistinguishable from simile:[24]

This is not to say that metaphor is the same as simile, an explicit assertion of a similarity. In 'the action of sleep on a careworn person is similar to the action of a knitter on a ravelled sleeve,' no expression is used metaphorically. Nevertheless, it remains true that the existence of such a similarity is presupposed by the metaphor. Thus, the difference between metaphor and simile is somewhat analogous to the difference between 'My son plays baseball' and 'I have a son and he plays baseball,' where what is presupposed but not explicitly asserted in the first is explicitly asserted in the second.

The formulaic approach thus presses its claims against intuitionism by (a) arguing that there must be operative principles underlying the metaphorical understanding and by (b) offering similarity as the basis of a principle peculiarly compatible with those creative aspects of metaphor emphasized by intuitionism. This principle contrasts sharply with those regularities relating the extensions of indicators to specified contextual features – each 'now', for example, denoting its own time period, each 'I' referring to its own producer.

The similarity principle underlying metaphor acquires determinacy only through appeal to relevant respects, since the respects in which any two things resemble one another are indefinitely large in number. To determine which of these are relevant is not, in general, a routine task. A fresh search of each context for what Alston describes as an 'important and readily noticeable similarity'[25] must be undertaken, with no advance limitation on the region within which such similarity may be located. No wonder that metaphorical interpretation never grows stale and is capable of yielding new insights with each probe into a fresh context.

The claim of the formulaic approach is, then, that the principle of similarity differs critically from the regularities governing indicator terms. Intuitionism's rejection of the formula thesis seems to depend on a blindness to such difference: Since metaphor is clearly irreducible to mere coinage and since, moreover, it eludes regularities of the indicator variety, it must be immune to all formula and based solely on special acts of metaphorical intuition. Once it is recognized that a similarity principle is peculiarly flexible, and dependent for its application on fresh contextual insight, the drive to intuition is halted and metaphor may be seen both as creative and as guided by formula.

The trouble, however, is that similarity yields a formula of only the weakest sort. It is indeed totally trivial if it specifies the meaning of a metaphorical expression by supplying a statement of bare similarity, any two things being similar in some respect or other. If the formula requires also that the respects in question be intended by the speaker, or (as Alston suggests) 'readily noticeable', it is inadequate to the full range of metaphorical expression, which often goes beyond intent and beneath the surface of the perceptibly salient.

If, finally, it is required that the similarity be an important one, the formula escapes vacuousness only by becoming heavily dependent on context: It tells us to search for important features of resemblance, the criteria of importance as well as the application of such criteria both to be supplied by the context in question. Any impression that the formulaic approach offers us a firm rule for decoding metaphors must evaporate upon learning that the rule in question requires a context-by-context selection of the very criteria by which decoding is to proceed. And the notion that such a rule explains the 'mechanics' of metaphor must founder with the realization that the mechanism operates through judgments of importance specific to varying contexts.

The deceptive simplicity of the formulaic approach is well illustrated by the appeal to iconicity referred to above. Henle's account appears to provide a straightforward analysis of metaphor: Semantically hybrid, metaphors operate first as symbols; things satisfying these symbols are then to be taken as icons of the object in question. 'The icon is never actually present; rather, through the rule, one understands what it must be and, through this understanding, what it signifies.'[26] Now the last and crucial step depends upon a judgment of similarity, since icons are presumed to signify by virtue of similarities to their respective objects. But the whole account thus loses its appearance of rule-governed simplicity, for the reasons outlined above.

In sum, the formulaic notion of metaphor as implicit simile is not persuasive. Transformation of the metaphorical 'Richard is a lion' into the literal 'Richard is like a lion' is indeed a simple operation, applicable as well to a wide array of statements. Yet, if the resulting simile is not to be interpreted as merely trivially true, it must be taken as appealing further to contextual criteria of importance. The formula turning metaphor into simile thus does not go far enough; it stops just short of providing a genuine illumination of either.

5 INTENSIONAL APPROACH TO METAPHOR

The *intensional* approach employs an idea already encountered in our treatment of emotivism – the idea that metaphorical effects are released through the blocking of normal interpretation. Emotivism, as we saw, held that metaphorical word combinations violate standing presumptions regarding the proper relations among terms, thus interrupting normal readings and allowing the emotive meaning of expressions to break through. Intensionalism employs the same general notion but it gives a cognitive rather than an emotive account of the metaphorical effect itself: It sees such effect not as a matter of feeling but rather as a genuine ascription of properties. However, its view is that, among the properties associated with a term, some are central while others are merely peripheral; when normal readings based on central properties are blocked, metaphorical readings emerge, based on compatible combinations of relevant peripheral properties.

Beardsley has developed a view of this sort, in which he distinguishes the characteristics *designated* by a word from those *connoted* by it; the former he takes as constituting the central, or primary meaning of the word, the latter as comprising its marginal, or secondary meanings. Designated characteristics are defining characteristics, whereas connoted characteristics are those not designated by the word in question but belonging, or 'widely thought or said to belong, to many of the things it denotes':[27]

> The word 'wolf', for example, designates certain characteristics that define a class of animals; it also *denotes* the animals that have those defining characteristics in common. But besides having the characteristics that make them wolves, many wolves have certain other characteristics, or are widely believed to have them: fierceness, persistence, and predatory clannishness. And these characteristics have been ascribed to wolves in contexts that contain the word 'wolf', whereas the contexts that contain its technical synonym, *Canis lupus*, have not so commonly ascribed such characteristics to them. Hence, when a person now uses the word 'wolf' in certain contexts,

we can infer that he probably believes that the entities referred to have some of the characteristics connoted by the term. And these characteristics, unless ruled out by the context, are part of what I call the full meaning of the word, though not of its strict, or dictionary, meaning – that is, its designation.

Connoted properties are latent unless released by the blocking of normal interpretation, which bases itself uniformly upon central, or designated, properties. Such blocking occurs through the violation of some standard presumption, e.g. the presumption of consistency, of concordance with contextual presuppositions, or of compatibility with obvious truths. 'To call a man a "fox" is indirectly self-contradictory because men are by definition bipeds and foxes quadrupeds, and it is logically impossible to be both.' Thus, the statement must, according to Beardsley, be taken as an example of metaphor: '"The man is a fox" says that the man has the characteristics connoted by "fox" . . .'.[28] He states his view (which he calls 'the Controversion Theory') in general terms as follows:[29]

> a metaphor is a significant attribution that is either indirectly self-contradictory or obviously false in its context, and in which the modifier connotes characteristics that can be attributed, truly or falsely, to the subject.

The metaphorical status of an expression is independent of the interpreter, according to Beardsley, for he writes:[30]

> The more difficult it is to work out connotations of the modifier that can be attributed to the subject, the more obscure is the metaphor – but this obviously depends upon the powers of the reader. As long as there are such connotations, it is still a metaphor, however obscure. But if there are no such connotations, we have not a metaphor, but *nonsense* of a particular kind.

As to the question which of the available connotations are to be assigned to the meaning of the metaphor in question, Beardsley replies that all are to be included provided consistency is not impaired:[31]

> The problem of construing the metaphor is that of deciding which of the modifier's connotations can *fit* the subject, and

the metaphor means *all* the connotations that can fit – except those that are further eliminated by, because they do not fit, the larger context.

Beardsley sums up the process of explicating metaphor in two principles: (a) '*The Principle of Congruence*', which tells us (in cases where normal interpretation is blocked) to apply to the subject only such connotations of the modifier as are fitting, i.e. as are logically and physically compatible with it ('in assembling . . . the admissible connotations of words in a poem, we are guided by logical and physical possibilities') and (b) '*The Principle of Plenitude*', which tells us that all fitting connotations are to be counted as belonging to the meaning of the metaphor, provided consistency is preserved throughout the context. Since he considers a metaphor to be 'a miniature poem, and the explication of a metaphor . . . a model of all explication', he applies his second principle to poetry as follows:[32]

All the connotations that can be found to fit are to be attributed to the poem: it means all it *can* mean, so to speak.

The two principles offered by Beardsley are intended to comprise a 'logic of explication'.[33] Beardsley writes, in a related passage, 'It may seem strange to apply to poetry the cold machinery of formal logic. But poetic statements, like all statements, have a logical form, and I am arguing that it is just their peculiarities of logical form on which their poetic power depends.'[34] Like the formulaic approach, which we have characterized as relying peculiarly upon a principle of similarity or resemblance, the intensional approach offers a *method* of interpretation. How does it, then, stand with reference to intuitionism? Does it, in particular, reject the anti-formula position?

The intuitionistic approach insists that there is no formula for deriving the meaning of a metaphor from the literal meanings of its constituents, and it rests ultimately, as we have suggested, upon a recognition of the role of ingenuity in the interpretation of metaphorical expressions. The intensional approach indeed offers a method but it does not purport to offer a formula of the sort rejected by intuitionism.

For one thing, the method operates not upon literal (i.e. 'primary') meanings, but upon connotative (i.e. 'secondary') meanings of constituents; moreover, these connotative meanings cannot be presumed to be immediately available to the interpreter: in principle, they require empirical search. For another thing, the connotative meanings determined to obtain cannot be directly applied to the subject; they require screening, not only for logical coherence but also for compatibility with physical laws. Finally, the method does not promise routinely to specify the metaphorical meaning of an expression; it offers only to guide the development of hypotheses as to such meaning. Different readers of a poem may, as Beardsley says:[35]

> work into it from different angles, so that each finds things the others have missed.... A proposed explication may be regarded as a hypothesis that is tested by its capacity to account for the greatest quantity of data in the words of the poem – including their potential connotations....

It is thus that intensionalism hopes to do justice both to the intuitionist opposition to formula, and to the insistence of the formulaic approach that metaphorical interpretation be explained as a principled process. Metaphor, as Beardsley puts it, 'augments the resources of our language. . . . But . . . metaphor is nevertheless analyzable.'[36]

6 EVALUATION OF INTENSIONALISM

Intensionalism, as explained by Beardsley, offers a comprehensive interpretation of metaphor that appears to escape the difficulties attaching to the approaches earlier considered. A strong point is its view of language as having layered interpretations, normal readings (based on primary meanings) taking precedence unless blocked through indirect self-contradiction or obvious falsehood, which releases the flow of secondary meanings. This idea of a hierarchy of readings (already encountered in emotivism and to be seen again in contextualism) persuasively pictures a typical background of metaphorical interpretation.

Two reservations must, however, be entered. The first is that a metaphorical reading may be prompted by some condition other than indirect self-contradiction or obvious falsehood. Some feature of intent or context may signal that an expression is to be read metaphorically, even though its normal literal interpretation is consistent and moreover true. Secondly, such a literal interpretation is not in every case superseded in favor of the metaphorical,[37] but is retained along with it as an instance of *multiple meaning* or what we referred to earlier as *M*-ambiguity.[38]

Before attempting a general evaluation of the intensional approach, I note three particular problems in Beardsley's account.[39] First, consider the reference to physical possibility. The key notion of indirect self-contradiction is initially introduced in terms of *logical* impossibility given relevant definitions, but the Principle of Congruence refers to *physical* as well as *logical* possibilities. This means, presumably, that a cluster of connotations may not be assigned to the subject of a metaphorical attribution if inconsistency results, given certain physical laws. The principle in question thus constrains the metaphorical explications offered at any time by what are considered physical laws at that time, irrespective of the belief status of such laws in the context of the metaphor's origination. What can justify such constraint?

Secondly, consider the reference to false metaphorical attributions. Beardsley's general formulation, cited above, states that the connotations of the modifier ascribed by a given metaphor to a subject are those 'that can be attributed, truly or falsely,' to it.[40] Now metaphor is activated, according to the view in question, when normal interpretation based upon central properties is blocked – and it is sufficient for this to occur that the normal reading is 'obviously false in its context'.[41] What, then, have we gained in allowing the metaphorical interpretation (based on connoted properties) to consist of false attributions, perhaps even obviously false attributions as well? In introducing the basic idea of his theory in connection with *self-contradiction* rather than *falsehood*, Beardsley writes:[42]

> when the modifier connotes some characteristic that can be meaningfully attributed to the subject, the reader jumps over the evident self-contradiction and construes it indirectly, on the principle that the writer knows he is contradicting himself and wouldn't utter anything at all unless he had something sensible in mind.

Here the 'evident self-contradiction' is traded for a 'meaningful' and 'sensible', though indirect, attribution; it would apparently not be an advantage here to offer an indirect but also self-contradictory attribution in place of the direct self-contradiction. Yet with respect to truth, Beardsley does not adopt the parallel attitude. Obvious falsehood may lead the reader to jump over the evident untruth and replace it by – any consistent attribution, true or false. Surely some qualification is required.

Thirdly, consider the question of the metaphor's independence of the interpreter. We noted Beardsley's insistence that, although a metaphor is difficult to interpret, 'as long as there are . . . connotations [of the modifier attributable to the subject], it is still a metaphor, however obscure'.[43] Whether there are connotations of the modifier logically and physically compatible with the subject (as Beardsley requires) is presumably a matter of fact independent not only of the interpreter but also of the author. This is apparently, too, a corollary of the Principle of Plenitude. Yet there are conflicting tendencies in Beardsley's account.

For example, the reader is said to jump over an *evident* self-contradiction, where possible, and to construe it indirectly, 'on the principle that the writer knows he is contradicting himself and wouldn't utter anything at all unless he had something sensible in mind'.[44] Apparently, the reader's construal is, among other things, to show how the utterance could have been produced by the author in question. By the suggested principle, therefore, this construal is constrained by what the author is considered to have had in mind at the time of origination of the utterance: Since every utterance presupposes a sensible something in the writer's mind at the time of its origination, non-sensible construals by the reader are ruled out. Once the constraint of the author's mind is introduced, however, how restrict it to the mere exclusion of the non-sensible? A particular writer's utterance will typically be thought to presuppose a *specific sort* of sensible something in mind at the time of origination. Does the reader then not need to ask, for each merely sensible construal that occurs to him, whether it is not perhaps ruled out by what the given author must be considered to have had in mind when he produced the utterance?

The case of metaphor, involving *indirect*, rather than *evident*, self-contradiction, seems parallel. Normal interpretation based on central properties is blocked, but why? We can *understand* inconsistent or obviously false utterances; why not interpret them normally and simply decide the utterances to be false? Presumably, we want not merely to understand the utterances but to understand how they could have been made, and normal interpretation fails on this score. That is why it is obvious falsehood that is thought to block normal interpretation, not just falsehood; a non-obvious or subtle untruth can be taken normally, producing no drive to metaphorical interpretation. But the effort to understand how a metaphor could have been made will not be hospitable to all consistent non-normal readings. By reference to the author's mind, it may be expected to select among these.

The need for an auxiliary selective principle is especially urgent for Beardsley's view, since the Principles of Congruence and Plenitude seem far too broad to provide guidance in interpretation: The notion of ascribing to the meaning of a metaphor all fitting connotations, provided consistency is preserved throughout, seems much too liberal to serve as a basis for the 'logic of explication'[45] that Beardsley seeks. A consideration of this problem will lead us to a general evaluation of the intensional approach.

Recall, to begin with, the contrast Beardsley makes between metaphor and nonsense. As long as there are connotations of the modifier consistently attributable to the subject, we have 'a metaphor, however obscure.' Without such connotations, 'we have not a metaphor, but *nonsense* of a particular kind.' Beardsley admits that it is not easy to find clear examples of nonsense; he further concedes that we cannot be sure a given attribution is nonsensical, 'because someone may find a meaning in it that we have overlooked.'[46] The fact is, however, that, given Beardsley's theory, no attribution is nonsensical. We can be sure of that since there is a simple routine for finding fitting connotations to enter into metaphorical meaning.

Let us take as our example the indirectly self-contradictory attribution 'John is a wolf', representing it schematically as 'Fa'. Now consider the property $x[Fx_v x=a]$, that is, the property of being an object x such that x is F or is identical with a. This property is connoted by 'F' since not a defining characteristic of it but clearly belonging to all the objects 'F' denotes. Being a wolf or identical with John characterizes all wolves whatever.

Hence it is, on Beardsley's account, connoted by 'wolf'; it is also consistently attributable to John. We need not, therefore, rely on the peculiar characteristics of 'fierceness, persistence, and predatory clannishness'[47] to save the indirectly self-contradictory 'John is a wolf' from nonsense, since our routinely constructed property suffices to guarantee metaphorical status and must, moreover, be counted as part of the relevant metaphorical meaning to be explicated. Analogous remarks hold when the indirectly self-contradictory attribution has a predicate in place of a name or singular description, e.g. 'FG' (for example, 'human wolf'); here the relevant property is $x[Fx_v Gx]$.

Now 'John is a wolf' and 'human wolf' are in any case treated as illustrative metaphors. However, Beardsley offers 'participial biped' and 'a man in the key of A flat' as 'very probably incapable of being explicated', i.e. as nonsense.[48] By the suggested routine, however, both these expressions must be counted as metaphorical, the first because 'participial' connotes the property of being participial or a biped, the second because 'in the key of A flat' connotes the property of being in the key of A flat or a man. I do not argue that the phrases in question really *are* nonsense, but only that the indicated properties give no basis for understanding them as metaphorical. Clearly the degree of latitude here sanctioned in the interpretation of metaphor is too great, and the Principles of Congruence and Plenitude admit too much.

Beardsley might, however, amend his theory, in a way designed to rule out troublesome properties of the sort discussed above, and so defend intensionalism against the criticism offered. He characterizes 'redundant' or 'tautological' attributions as 'self-implicative' and considers them *logically empty* or *logically absurd*, since 'the meaning of the modifier is already contained in the meaning of the subject'.[49] He might, accordingly, narrow his notion of connotation so as to exclude the property of being a wolf or identical with John from the connotation of 'wolf', since the attribution 'Every wolf is a wolf or identical with John' is self-implicative. (Analogously, being participial or a biped would be excluded from the connotation of 'participial', since yielding the self-implicative attribution 'Everything that is participial is participial or a biped.' Etc.) As an alternative amendment, such properties might be retained within their original respective ranges of *connotation*, but excluded from relevant metaphorical *explications*; this would amount to a restriction of the Principle of Plenitude. Thus, the property of being participial or a biped, though recognized as part of the connotation of 'participial', would now be barred from the metaphorical meaning of 'participial' in the attribution 'participial biped' on the ground that the explicative phrase 'biped that is participial or a biped' is self-implicative. (Similarly for 'wolf', the property of being a wolf or identical with John, and the self-implicative explication 'John is a wolf or identical with John', etc.)

The amended doctrine is nevertheless still too broad to ground a logic of metaphorical explication. Consider again 'John is a wolf' and assume that such properties as being a wolf or identical with John, being a wolf or an automobile or identical with John, etc., have been successfully eliminated by amendment on grounds of self-implication, as suggested. There remain indefinitely many connotations (aside from Beardsley's favored 'fierceness, persistence, and predatory clannishness') that are treated by amended intensionalism as belonging to the metaphorical meaning of 'wolf' in the attribution in question, but that can hardly be accepted as such.

Recall that the characteristics connoted by a word are described as those 'that it does not designate but that belong, or are widely thought or said to belong, to many of the things it denotes.'[50] For 'wolf', this description fits, e.g. the characteristic of not being a tree, the characteristic of not being identical with Aristotle, that of being located within our solar system, that of having eyes, of occupying space, of being larger than a mushroom, and so forth. To say of John that he is larger than a mushroom is not self-implicative, but it is hardly plausible to suppose that 'John is a wolf' contains this ascription as part of its metaphorical meaning. Nor do the Principles of Congruence and Plenitude offer a convincing 'method, or logic'[51] of explication if they yield indefinitely many ascriptions of the sort here illustrated.

Even the attributions that Beardsley supposes 'very probably incapable of being explicated' i.e. 'participial biped' and 'a man in the key of A flat', qualify as metaphorical in virtue of connotations admitted by *amended* intensionalism. For nothing participial is a rhinoceros or a palm tree, and everything participial has an origin postdating the formation of the earth; each of these characteristics is, moreover, consistent (logically and physically) with being a biped. Everything in the key of A flat is a non-elephant, is perceivable by the senses, and has a temporal span of less than 200 years; each of these characteristics is consistently attributable to men. Yet it can hardly be claimed that the above connotations, uneliminated by appeal to self-implication, provide a basis for interpreting the attributions in question as metaphorical.

Are not such connotations eliminable, however, on grounds of *obviousness*, if not on grounds of *self-implication*? For is it not *obviously* (if not *logically*) true that John is larger than a mushroom, that no biped is a rhinoceros, that no man lives for 200 years? Why not then (by a further amendment) either exclude the troublesome properties from the range of *connotation* (since e.g. 'Every wolf is larger than a mushroom' is obviously true), or exclude them from explications of metaphorical meaning (since, e.g. the explicative phrase 'biped that is not a palm tree' is *obviously*, if not *logically*, redundant and the explicative sentence 'John is larger than a mushroom' is obviously true)?

It is a defect of this suggestion that it rests on the elusive notion of obviousness. But further clarification is not in point for the proposed amendment is in any case fruitless. Under any likely interpretation of 'obvious', there will be indefinitely many non-obvious characteristics of wolves, consistently and non-obviously attributable to John, but difficult to assign to the relevant metaphorical meaning. Wolves have, say, a certain anatomical or physiological property, G, and men have another, M, both having been discovered through specialized laboratory research and unknown to the public at large. The property of having G or M is, then, a non-obvious connotation of 'wolf' since it is true – but neither logically nor obviously so – that this non-designated characteristic of 'wolf' in fact belongs to all wolves. Further, the property in question is also attributable, consistently and non-obviously, to John, it being equally true, but not obviously so, that John has G or M. Yet can it be seriously supposed that having G or M is part of the metaphorical meaning of 'wolf' in the attribution 'John is a wolf'? Can the task of metaphorical explication include providing a detailed account of the properties of wolves' neural structures or blood chemistry?

The excessive breadth of intensionalism evidently arises from the fact that its basic notion of 'connotation' comprehends not only the (non-designated) characteristics *thought to* belong to a term's denotata, but also those *in fact* belonging to them.[52] And the explicative apparatus built on this notion is too inclusive for the task at hand. The Principle of Congruence, appealing merely to consistency among such connotations, is too weak to rule out the unwanted ones among them; the Principle of Congruence positively requires them to be included. Is there any way of tightening the interpretive apparatus of intensionalism so as to provide stronger guidance, without incurring again the difficulties of the formulaic approach? This is one promise of the interactional view, to which we now turn.

7   INTERACTIONISM AND METAPHOR

The *interactional* approach agrees with Intuitionism in denying that metaphorical interpretation can be reduced to some general routine, but it does not rest content with appeal to the act of intuition. Denying that metaphors operate solely or primarily in the realm of feeling, it differs sharply from the emotive approach. Like the formulaic and the intensional approaches, interactionism seeks rather a cognitive interpretation of metaphorical understanding. However, unlike the first of these approaches, it rejects the association of metaphor with simile, as well as all appeals to resemblance and comparison. And unlike the second, it gives up the inclusive notion of a term's connotations as embracing both the ('non-designated') characteristics in fact belonging to its denotata and the characteristics thought to belong to them. In focusing upon the latter sort alone, interactionism promises to remedy the difficulty of excessive breadth, to which intensionalism is vulnerable.

Max Black presents an interactional view, elaborated upon a basis in I. A. Richards's *The Philosophy of Rhetoric*. Black quotes Richards's statement:[53]

> In the simplest formulation, when we use a metaphor we have two thoughts of different things active together and supported by a single word, or phrase, whose meaning is a resultant of their interaction.

Black understands this statement to imply that the metaphorical term (in his terminology, the 'focus' of the metaphor) acquires 'a new meaning, which is not quite its meaning in literal uses, nor quite the meaning which any literal substitute would have.' The context of the metaphorical term (as Black refers to it, the 'frame') produces an extension of meaning in the focal term. 'And', writes Black, 'I take Richards to be saying that for the metaphor to work the reader must remain aware of the extension of meaning – must attend to both the old and the new meanings together.'[54]

How is the extension of meaning produced? Black attempts to make the process clearer by going beyond Richards' description in terms of the 'interaction' of two thoughts 'active together', of ideas 'which co-operate in an inclusive meaning.'[55] He writes as follows:[56]

> Let us try, for instance, to think of a metaphor as a filter. Consider the statement, 'Man is a wolf.' Here, we may say, are *two* subjects – the principal subject, Man (or: men) and the subsidiary subject, Wolf (or: wolves). Now the metaphorical sentence in question will not convey its intended meaning to a reader sufficiently ignorant about wolves. What is needed is not so much that the reader shall know the standard dictionary meaning of 'wolf' – or be able to use that word in literal senses – as that he shall know what I will call the *system of associated commonplaces*. Imagine some layman required to say, without taking special thought, those things he held to be true about wolves; the set of statements resulting would approximate to what I am here calling the system of commonplaces associated with the word 'wolf'.

It is assumed that such systems of commonplaces are relatively uniform throughout any given culture; it is also assumed that they typically include 'half-truths' and 'downright mistakes'. As Black emphasizes, 'the important thing for the metaphor's effectiveness is not that the commonplaces shall be true, but that they should be readily and freely evoked.'[57]

To call a man a wolf is, in fact, 'to evoke the wolf-system of related commonplaces':[58]

If the man is a wolf, he preys upon other animals, is fierce, hungry, engaged in constant struggle, a scavenger, and so on. Each of these implied assertions has now to be made to fit the principal subject (the man) either in normal or in abnormal senses. . . . A suitable hearer will be led by the wolf-system of implications to construct a corresponding system of implications about the principal subject.

These latter implications will, however, not be found among the commonplaces associated with 'man', but rather determined by those associated with 'wolf'. The effect is to make salient those features of man that can be described by 'wolf'-commonplaces. 'Any human traits that can without undue strain be talked about in "wolf-language" will be rendered prominent, and any that cannot will be pushed into the background. The wolf-metaphor suppresses some details, emphasizes others – in short, *organizes* our view of man.'[59]

Black offers another analogy. Looking at the sky at night through a 'smoked glass on which certain lines have been left clear',[60]

I shall see only the stars that can be made to lie on the lines previously prepared upon the screen, and the stars I do see will be seen as organized by the screen's structure. We can think of a metaphor as such a screen and the system of 'associated commonplaces' of the focal word as the network of lines upon the screen. We can say that the principal subject is 'seen through' the metaphorical expression . . .

Summarizing the features of the interaction view, Black enumerates seven points: (1) a metaphorical statement has two subjects, a principal and a subsidiary one; (2) these are 'often best regarded as "systems of things" rather than "things"'; (3) a metaphor applies to its principal subject a system of 'associated implications' belonging to its subsidiary subject; (4) while such implications usually consist of commonplaces, they may on occasion 'consist of deviant implications established *ad hoc* by the writer'; (5) a metaphor selects and organizes features of the principal subject by 'implying statements about it that normally apply to the subsidiary subject'; (6) such implication involves shifts in the meaning of words 'belonging to the same family or system as the metaphorical expression; and some of these shifts, though not all, may be metaphorical transfers'; and (7) 'there is, in general, no simple "ground" for the necessary shifts of meaning – no blanket reason why some metaphors work and others fail.'[61]

8   EVALUATION OF INTERACTIONISM

The interactional view provides an elaborate set of ideas for the interpretation of metaphor and, as already suggested, seems to have a clear advantage over intensionalism in its more restricted conception of transferred characteristics. We shall, however, reserve for the end of the section a discussion of the problem of excessive breadth, and begin here with a consideration of the central notion of interaction.

In what respects is there thought to be a reciprocity of influence between the elements believed to interact? The implication-system of the subsidiary subject organizes our view of the principal subject but is itself altered in the process. 'The nature of the intended application helps to determine the character of the system to be applied. . . .'[62] To call a man a wolf, for example, is to evoke the normal wolf-system of implications, to be transferred to the man in question. Some of these implications may be transferred directly without difficulty; others require stretching or shifting of meaning. 'Each . . . has now to be made to fit the principal subject (the man) either in normal or in abnormal senses.'[63] The implications in question thus shape our notion of the man while themselves subject to meaning change in the process of application.

Does the interaction here outlined suffer from circularity or the threat of infinite regress, purporting to explain metaphorical meaning change through appeal to further metaphorical meaning change? Black himself alerts us to the objection: 'The primary metaphor, it might be said, has been analyzed into a set of subordinate metaphors, so the account given is either circular or leads to an infinite regress.' He offers two replies. First, not all shifts of meaning in the commonplaces are metaphorical shifts. Many, he says, 'are best described as extensions of meaning, because they do not involve apprehended connections between two systems of concepts.' He continues:[64]

I have not undertaken to explain how such extensions or shifts occur in general, and I do not think any simple account will fit all cases. (It is easy enough to mutter 'analogy', but closer examination soon shows all kinds of 'grounds' for shifts of meaning with context – and even no ground at all, sometimes.)

Secondly, Black allows that a metaphor may indeed include subordinate metaphors among its implications, these 'usually intended to be taken less "emphatically", i.e. with less stress upon their implications.'[65] So long as not all the meaning changes in question are metaphorical, and – a point Black overlooks – so long as each metaphorical change is explainable ultimately without appealing to further metaphorical change, the danger of circularity or infinite regress is avoided.

The situation is thus to be pictured as follows: To call a man a wolf is to produce a metaphorical change of meaning in the focal word 'wolf': 'The new context . . . imposes extension of meaning upon the focal word.'[66] Such change is explained by reference to transfer of the wolf-system of implications to the man involved. Certain of these implications (or, to simplify, their ingredient predicates) may be transferred directly, that is to say, without meaning change at all. (E.g. 'fierce' may perhaps be suggested here.) Others require non-metaphorical extensions of meaning to fit (e.g. 'preys upon other animals', perhaps.) Still others undergo metaphorical changes of meaning and (as I have suggested) each such change must itself be explainable by the very process of implication-transfer invoked above for 'wolf', but terminable in a finite number of analogously repeated steps without ultimate appeal to metaphorical meaning change.

Thus if 'hungry', for example, is considered to undergo *metaphorical* change of meaning when transferred from wolves to men, we must inquire into *its* system of associated implications. Suppose 'unsatisfied' and 'driven' are the sole predicates belonging to this system, 'unsatisfied' transferring directly and 'driven' transferring through non-metaphorical extension; 'hungry' is in this case explainable as a metaphorically changed attribution to men, and in turn helps to explain the metaphorical attribution of 'wolf' itself. So long as all metaphorical changes (primary or subordinate) are explained by chains of transfer finitely terminable in direct transfers or non-metaphorical meaning changes taken as primitive, the procedure avoids circularity and infinite regress.

Still, the total picture is unsatisfying; in particular, the appeal to unexplained meaning changes in the account of metaphor must be considered a serious limitation. It will be recalled that Black began by proposing to go beyond Richards' apparent appeal to the notion of a meaning extension. 'How', Black had asked, 'is this extension or change of meaning brought about?'[67] We now find that this question, if somewhat reduced in scope, remains applicable to his own interpretation. For, though he discourses freely of meaning changes, he provides no general account.

Nor is it easy, given the general picture under discussion, to see why Black supposes that 'interaction-metaphors' are 'not expendable' – why, that is, they must be expected to lose cognitive content in translation. He writes:[68]

> Suppose we try to state the cognitive content of an interaction-metaphor in 'plain language'. Up to a point, we may succeed in stating a number of the relevant relations between the two subjects (though in view of the extension of meaning accompanying the shift in the subsidiary subject's implication system, too much must not be expected of the literal paraphrase). But the set of literal statements so obtained will not have the same power to inform and enlighten as the original. For one thing, the implications, previously left for a suitable reader to educe for himself, with a nice feeling for their relative priorities and degrees of importance, are now presented explicitly as though having equal weight. The literal paraphrase inevitably says too much – and with the wrong emphasis. One of the points I most wish to stress is that the loss in such cases is a loss in cognitive content; the relevant weakness of the literal paraphrase is not that it may be tiresomely prolix or boringly explicit (or deficient in qualities of style); it fails to be a translation because it fails to give the insight that the metaphor did.

Now the metaphorical meaning change of the focal word (say, 'wolf') is to be interpreted by reference to the transfer of wolf-implications to the relevant principal subject (say, man). Some such implications transfer directly, that is to say, without meaning change at all; these are, presumably, literal. Other such implications involve primitive (i.e. unexplained) extensions of meaning in the process of transfer. These extensions, though deviating from the literal, are however, *as Black himself insists*, not metaphorical either. Finally, certain implications undergo metaphorical change in transfer. But each of these (as I have earlier suggested) is itself to be regarded as finitely terminating in direct (literal), transferred implications or in primitively shifted (non-metaphorical), implications. Thus every one of the transferred implications of the original metaphor is formulable in non-metaphorical (though not always literal) terms.

Black argues generally that the literal paraphrase of a metaphor 'fails to be a translation because it fails to give the insight that the metaphor did.' Translation, however, is a variable notion and construing it so as to require equivalence of insight yields a strong version likely to be vacuous in any case. Given such a construction, no statement – literal or metaphorical – is expendable. On the other hand, if a weaker notion of translation permits paraphrase anywhere without 'loss in cognitive content', Black's argument gives no reason for denying that interaction-metaphors may be thus paraphrased in literal terms.

Turning now to the issue of explicating metaphors, let us reconsider the problem of excessive breadth that plagued intensionalism. For it was here that we noted a likely advantage of the interactional approach, in its more restricted conception of transferred characteristics.

Recall that the problem arises for intensionalism because its notion of 'connotation' includes not only the characteristics *thought to* belong to a term's denotata, but also the characteristics *in fact* belonging to them. Now interactionism focuses upon the former sort exclusively, thus promising to escape the problem. The system of implications transferred from subsidiary to principal subject does not embrace all the (non-designated) characteristics in fact belonging to a term's denotata. It may, on occasion, contain 'deviant implications established *ad hoc* by the writer',[69] but typically comprises just commonplaces, that is, 'those things . . . held to be true' about the relevant subject by laymen, as a matter of common belief within the culture in question. 'The effect, then, of (metaphorically) calling a man a "wolf" is to evoke the wolf-system of related commonplaces.'[70]

Clearly, the problem of non-obvious characteristics that caused difficulty for intensionalism is no problem for the interactional approach. That having G or M is in fact a characteristic of all wolves does not in itself imply that it enters into the metaphorical meaning of 'John is a wolf'. For metaphorical relevance, inter-actionism requires further that the characteristic be commonly held to be a property of wolves, or that it be established *ad hoc* by the writer as a property to be ascribed to wolves in the context in question. The job of metaphorical explication is thus suitably limited, concentrating on commonly held beliefs concerning denotata of the metaphorical term, and sensitive also to deviant assumptions of the author that may be salient in context.

Although interactionism thus escapes the difficulty of non-obvious characteristics, it seems still subject to the earlier difficul-ties of intensionalism with *obvious* characteristics. For these do not merely belong in fact to the relevant denotata, but do so obviously, that is, are commonly held to do so. They thus not only comprise *connotations* for intensionalism; they also enter into the *commonplaces* referred to by interactionism. That wolves are larger than mushrooms is not only true but also commonly held to be true by laymen within our culture. These laymen also normally hold that wolves have eyes, occupy space and have weight; they are persuaded that no wolf is a tree or an umbrella or identical with Mount Everest. Does interactionism then imply that to call men wolves is to say that men too are larger than mushrooms, have eyes, and so forth?

The answer is no. For Black requires that, in the transfer of wolf-implications to men, such implications do not already figure as commonplaces of 'man'. He writes:[71]

A suitable hearer will be led by the wolf-system of implications to construct a corresponding system of implications about the principal subject. But these implications will *not* be those comprised in the commonplaces *normally* implied by literal uses of 'man'. The new implications must be determined by the pattern of implications associated with literal uses of the word 'wolf'.

Now each of the obvious characteristics in the examples under discussion is commonly held to belong not only to wolves but also to men; it is generally believed not only of wolves but of men that they have eyes, occupy space, and are larger than mushrooms. Thus the metaphorical transfer from wolves to men excludes these characteristics. Interactionism requires, in short, that the transferred characteristics be obvious relative to the subsidiary subject, but non-obvious relative to the principal subject. It is because fierceness is *not* obvious relative to men that its ascription via the metaphorical attribution of 'wolf' produces a reorganization of viewpoint; it promises a novel truth.

Interactionism thus seems indeed to avoid the difficulties of excessive breadth that have so far been discussed. Requiring that transferred characteristics be obvious relative to the subsidiary subject, it surmounts the problem exemplified by the property of having G or M. Requiring that transferred characteristics be also non-obvious relative to the principal subject, it overcomes the difficulty illustrated by such characteristics as being larger than a mushroom. It does not follow, however, that interactionism is therefore adequate.

It seems in fact still too broad to illuminate the metaphorical transfer of characteristics from subsidiary to principal subject. For among the characteristics commonly held to belong to wolves is the characteristic of having four legs, which is also non-obvious relative to men. Yet clearly *this* characteristic is not transferred to men by the metaphor, 'Men are wolves'. The requirement of non-obviousness may however be strengthened so that any characteristic to be transferred must be not only (i) not commonly ascribed to the principal subject, but also (ii) not commonly denied of the principal subject. The characteristic of having four legs (with men as principal subject) satisfies condition (i) but not condition (ii); thus it is not subject to transfer.

It is, however, commonly believed of wolves that they do not speak French, while this characteristic is neither commonly ascribed to men (as is being larger than a mushroom) nor commonly denied of them (as is having four legs). Yet it seems clear that 'men are wolves' does not transfer the property of not speaking French from subsidiary to principal subject. Nor does 'John is a wolf' (assuming it is not generally believed of John that he does or that he does not speak French) promise to reorganize our view of him by affirming that he is not a French speaker. (And should it be suggested that there is no transfer in the case of 'Men are wolves', because, while the property in question is not commonly ascribed to all men, it is ascribed to most, consideration of the property of not being able to whistle a tune, commonly denied of most men, and of such properties as having sharp teeth or liking to eat the meat of sheep, properties which I suggest are neither commonly ascribed to nor denied of most men – will dispel the suggestion.)

Black says of the wolf-metaphor, 'Any human traits that can without undue strain be talked about in "wolf-language" will be rendered prominent, and any that cannot will be pushed into the background. The wolf-metaphor . . . *organizes* our view of man.'[72] In the examples just considered we have human traits that can easily be talked about in 'wolf-language', but they are surely not rendered prominent nor do they help to organize our view of man. The interactional approach thus seems also vulnerable to the difficulty of excessive breadth.

Are there any remedies available to the interactionist? Conceivably, the notion of a *commonplace* might be constricted so as to embrace only what is *spontaneously* offered as a statement of belief, thus ruling out e.g. the belief that wolves do not speak French or whistle tunes. Such an idea is suggested by Black in writing, 'Imagine some layman required to say, without taking special thought, those things he held to be true about wolves; the set of statements resulting would approximate to what I am here calling the system of commonplaces associated with the word "wolf"'.[73]

This remedy conflicts, however, with another criterion Black offers. Literal uses of words normally commit the speaker, he says, to sets of standard beliefs current in the speech community.[74]

> To deny any such piece of accepted commonplace (e.g. by saying that wolves are vegetarians – or easily domesticated) is to produce an effect of paradox and provoke a demand for justification. A speaker who says 'wolf' is normally taken to be implying in some sense of that word that he is referring to something fierce, carnivorous, treacherous, and so on.

Applying this test, we get a result that conflicts with the spontaneity criterion. For surely to deny that wolves do not speak French or to assert that they can whistle a tune is to produce an effect of paradox and to provoke a demand for justification. If this is the test to be used, then in saying 'wolf' the speaker must be held normally to imply not only a reference to something fierce and treacherous but also a reference to something that does not speak French or whistle tunes.

Moreover, the spontaneity test itself admits such characteristics as, for example, having sharp teeth, fearing fire, and running fast – characteristics that satisfy conditions (i) and (ii) above. Yet the assertion 'John is a wolf' does not say of John that he dreads fire and runs fast, nor does 'Men are wolves' organize our dental conception of man. I conclude that interactionism also gives an inadequate account of metaphorical explication, owing to its excessive breadth. It purports to tell us how metaphors organize our view of certain things, but the described mode of organization is insufficiently selective to account for the practice of explication.

There is also a problem of excessive narrowness. While Black introduces the interactional view by describing the role of *commonplaces*, he summarizes the main features of this view by referring rather to *implications*. 'These implications', he says, 'usually consist of "commonplaces" about the subsidiary subject, but may, in suitable cases, consist of deviant implications established *ad hoc* by the writer.'[75] He explains:[76]

> Reference to 'associated commonplaces' will fit the commonest cases where the author simply plays upon the stock of common knowledge (and common misinformation) presumably shared by the reader and himself. But in a poem, or a piece of sustained prose, the writer can establish a novel pattern of implications for the literal uses of the key expressions, prior to using them as vehicles for his metaphors. . . . Metaphors can be supported by specially constructed systems of implications, as well as by accepted commonplaces; they can be made to measure and need not be reach-me-downs.

A formulation of interactionism in terms of commonplaces alone is thus not only too broad but also too narrow, for it excludes metaphors based upon deviant implications established in context. We can see, in retrospect, that such narrowness affects intensionalism as well. For intensionalism rests upon ascription to the subject of the modifier's connotations, these connotations consisting of properties belonging, or widely thought to belong, to many denotata of the modifier. Metaphors resting upon deviant features, that is to say, upon features neither belonging, nor widely thought to belong, to the modifier's denotata but established by the author as relevant in context, are excluded.

Black's summary statement of interactionism refers, as we have seen, not to commonplaces but rather to implications, said *'usually'* to consist of commonplaces but also *'in suitable cases'* to consist of deviant implications. This formulation is meant to eliminate the defect of excessive narrowness we have mentioned, but it does so only through incorporation of an appeal to context. When are commonplaces to be taken to rule, and when, alternatively, are deviant implications rather to be assumed to govern? Some judgment of the context is implicitly presupposed as available to decide and, further, to determine the particular deviant implications in question. Interactionism here verges on contextualism, which we shall consider next.

9   CONTEXTUALISM AND METAPHOR

The *contextual* approach gives primary emphasis to a feature of metaphorical understanding that is noted by other views as well and, as we have recently seen, by interactionism in particular – the reference to context. Contextualism is cognitive in spirit, thus differing from emotivism; it differs, further, from the formulaic approach in rejecting reliance on resemblance and from the intensional approach in rejecting a logic of explication based upon uniform principles of interpretation. Like interactionism, it is prepared to recognize that metaphorical ascription varies in its force with variation in context, but it offers no theory of commonplaces even as a presumptive account of the usual case.

In placing primary emphasis on contextual variation, it has clear affinities with intuitionism, which stresses the role of ingenuity in each instance of metaphorical understanding. But it does not purport to offer an explanation of metaphor in terms of intuitive acts of the mind. Rather, it suggests that a search of the context of each metaphor yields, in favorable cases, a set of cues relevant to its interpretation; such cues may remove the local mystery, even if no general principles of explication hold across contexts.

A contextual approach is suggested by the treatment of

metaphor offered by Nelson Goodman. A review of the general features of his treatment will facilitate appreciation of its contextual character. Metaphor, he says, 'is a matter of teaching an old word new tricks – of applying an old label in a new way.'[77] This characterization is, however, not sufficient, since 'every application of a predicate to a new event or a new-found object is new; but such routine projection does not constitute metaphor.' The further characterization offered is as follows:[78]

> In routine projection, habit applies a label to a case not already decided. Arbitrary application of a newly coined term is equally unobstructed by prior decision. But metaphorical application of a label to an object defies an explicit or tacit prior denial of that label to that object. Where there is metaphor, there is conflict: the picture is sad rather than gay even though it is insentient and hence neither sad nor gay. Application of a term is metaphorical only if to some extent contra-indicated.

However, metaphorical truth, as distinct from simple falsehood, requires further that there be 'attraction as well as resistance – indeed, an attraction that overcomes resistance.'[79] To describe the picture as sad is to offer a true characterization capable of surviving conflict with the picture's insentience, which implies that it is not sad. 'Nothing can be both sad and not sad unless "sad" has two different ranges of application. If the picture is (literally) not sad and yet is (metaphorically) sad, "sad" is used first as a label for certain sentient things or events, and then for certain insentient ones.'[80] How is metaphor then distinguished from ambiguity, also characterized by different ranges of application for a given term?[81]

> Applying the term 'cape' to a body of land on one occasion and to an article of clothing on another is using it with different and indeed mutually exclusive ranges but is not in either case metaphorical. How, then, do metaphor and ambiguity differ? Chiefly, I think, in that the several uses of a merely ambiguous term are coeval and independent; none either springs from or is guided by another. In metaphor, on the other hand, a term with an extension established by habit is applied elsewhere under the influence of that habit; there is both departure from and deference to precedent. When one use of a term precedes and informs another, the second is the metaphorical one.

The process by which one use of a term 'guides' or 'informs' another requires further interpretation. Goodman introduces the notions of 'schema' and 'realm', a schema consisting in a set of alternative labels, and a realm consisting of 'the objects sorted by the schema – that is, of the objects denoted by at least one of the alternative labels.' The underlying point is that:[82]

> a label functions not in isolation but as belonging to a family. We categorize by sets of alternatives. Even constancy of literal application is usually relative to a set of labels: what counts as red, for example, will vary somewhat depending upon whether objects are being classified as red or nonred, or as red or orange or yellow or green or blue or violet. What the admitted alternatives are is of course less often determined by declaration than by custom and context.

Now in metaphor, says Goodman, we typically see a change in the realm of a label as well as a change in its range or extension.[83]

> A label along with others constituting a schema is in effect detached from the home realm of that schema and applied for the sorting and organizing of an alien realm. Partly by thus carrying with it a reorientation of a whole network of labels does a metaphor give clues for its own development and elaboration.

The suggestion here is that the new application of a metaphorical label is guided, in part, by its place in the whole schema, which is itself transferred in a way that reflects its prior use:[84]

> a set of terms, of alternative labels, is transported; and the organization they effect in the alien realm is guided by their habitual use in the home realm.

As to how such guidance operates, Goodman offers no general account. He emphasizes the fact that the free transfer of a schema nevertheless yields determinate judgments:[85]

> We may at will apply temperature-predicates to sounds or hues or personalities or to degrees of nearness to a correct answer; but *which* elements in the chosen realm are warm, or are warmer than others is then very largely determinate. Even where a schema is imposed upon a most unlikely and uncongenial

realm, antecedent practice channels the application of the labels.

This is, however, just to describe the main phenomenon that has concerned us, i.e. the success that may accompany metaphorical communication. Granted that freely transferred schemata yield determinate judgments, the problem is to explain how. It is Goodman's response to this problem that I interpret as suggesting a contextual approach. For he resolutely resists the provision of a general answer, offering instead illustrations of a variety of metaphoric processes.

Thus he suggests that the guidance given by past uses may, in certain cases, derive not from the literal but from the metaphorical applications of the term in question:[86]

> perhaps, for instance, the way we apply 'high' to sounds was guided by the earlier metaphorical application to numbers (via number of vibrations per second) rather than directly by the literal application according to altitude.

Further, he suggests that guidance may derive not only from the past applications of a label, whether literal or metaphorical, but also from its past exemplifications (literal or metaphorical). In this connection, he refers to E. H. Gombrich's game of 'ping' and 'pong'. The object of the game is to apply these nonsense words to pairs of objects, and the result for many pairs is surprisingly determinate. Gombrich writes:[87]

> If these [words] were all we had and we had to name an elephant and a cat, which would be ping and which pong? I think the answer is clear. Or hot soup and ice cream. To me, at least, ice cream is ping and soup pong. Or Rembrandt and Watteau? Surely in that case Rembrandt would be pong and Watteau ping.

The guidance underlying the determinate responses in these examples cannot derive from the past denotation of the words in question, since they have had no denotation at all. Goodman's idea is that they have, however, exemplified certain properties or predicates, and that they now take over the denotation of the latter:[88]

The application of these words looks back not to how they

have been used to classify anything but to how they have
themselves been classified – not to what they antecedently
denote but to what they antecedently exemplify. We apply
'ping' to quick, light, sharp things, and 'pong' to slow, heavy,
dull things because 'ping' and 'pong' exemplify these properties.

Since 'ping' and 'pong' have had no prior denotation, there can
of course be no metaphor involved in their new applications in
the game. But guidance by past exemplification may also affect
the reassignment of a denoting label, and here the effect will be
metaphorical.

Still, the foregoing suggestions do not account for all cases or,
indeed, for all relevant aspects of metaphorical transfer. That
guidance derives from a prior metaphorical application may help
explain the present metaphor (as an elliptical instance of such
application), but hardly the earlier one. That exemplification may
play a role is illuminating, but in the case of 'ping' and 'pong' at
least, it is *metaphorical* exemplification that is presupposed: 'ping'
is not literally light and sharp, nor is 'pong' literally heavy and
dull; such cases assume certain metaphors in explaining others.
Further, the primary case of guidance through past literal
applications is itself assumed but not explained.

Goodman himself, having given us his account of the directive
effect of past exemplifications, continues as follows:[89]

The mechanism of transfer is often much less transparent.
Why does 'sad' apply to certain pictures and 'gay' to others?
What is meant by saying that a metaphorical application is
'guided by' or 'patterned after' the literal one? Sometimes
we can contrive a plausible history: warm colors are those of
fire, cold colors those of ice. In other cases we have only
fanciful alternative legends. Did numbers come to be higher
and lower because piles grow higher as more stones are put on
(despite the fact that holes go lower as more shovelfuls are
taken out)? Or were numerals inscribed on tree trunks from
the ground upward? Whatever the answer, these are all isolated
questions of etymology.

Etymological or not, such occasionally 'plausible histories'
suitable to their respective contexts are all that Goodman offers
to supplement the incomplete prior account of metaphoric pro-

cesses. Can anything more be provided? 'Presumably', he writes, 'we are being asked, rather, for some general account of how metaphorical use of a label reflects its literal use.' He admits that there has been 'suggestive speculation' on this question, referring, for illustration, to the view that the literal use of many terms has been narrowed from an initially wider range, an apparently new metaphorical application being thus often merely a recovery of the earlier territory. Nevertheless he concludes that such a view 'obviously does not explain the metaphorical applications of all or even most terms. Only rarely can the adult adventures of a label be thus traced back to childhood deprivations.'[90]

We have then an incomplete account of various processes operative in metaphoric transfer, and a suggestion of various plausible histories, together with the intimation that additional histories may be produced for individual contexts. Beyond that, Goodman maintains that no general theory of guidance can be offered. In particular, no general answer is to be sought in the notion of similarity:[91]

> Is saying that a picture is sad saying elliptically that it is like a sad person? . . . But the simile cannot amount merely to saying that the picture is like the person in some respect or other; anything is like anything else to that extent. What the simile says in effect is that person and picture are alike in being sad, the one literally and the other metaphorically. Instead of metaphor reducing to simile, simile reduces to metaphor; or rather, the difference between simile and metaphor is negligible. Whether the locution be 'is like' or 'is', the figure *likens* picture to person by picking out a certain common feature: that the predicate 'sad' applies to both, albeit to the person initially and to the picture derivatively.

Is there, then, no general sort of similarity between the things a term applies to literally and the things it applies to metaphorically? Goodman suggests the same question might well be asked about the things a term applies to literally. In what way must all (literally) green things, for example, be similar?[92]

> Having some property or other in common is not enough; they must have a *certain* property in common. But what property? Obviously the property named by the predicate in

question; that is, the predicate must apply to all the things it must apply to. The question why predicates apply as they do metaphorically is much the same as the question why they apply as they do literally. And if we have no good answer in either case, perhaps that is because there is no real question.

10   EVALUATION OF CONTEXTUALISM

It is perhaps worth noting that Goodman's use of 'metaphor' (like that of a good deal of the relevant literature), vacillates between a very broad interpretation, in which it covers virtually all figures of speech, and a narrow interpretation, in which it represents a figure closely akin to simile. The general notion of schematic transfer covers a wide variety of figurative expressions and Goodman indeed proposes an organization of this variety in a section of his discussion entitled 'Modes of Metaphor'.[93] On the other hand, in his criticism of the theory of metaphor as elliptical simile, he rejects the reduction of the former to the latter in favor of the view (quoted above) that 'the difference between simile and metaphor is negligible'. The ambiguity deserves attention but is perhaps theoretically harmless once remarked. Figurative expressions may well be profitably treated as a group under the heading of schematic transfer; those of the group with relatively clear bases of transfer having been segregated, the particularly difficult remainder associated with simile wants special attention and has, indeed, been the focus of most theoretical discussions. Our own initial characterizations of metaphor were based on the broad interpretation, while our discussions of various theorists have followed their lead in frequently assuming a narrower reading.

A basic question about Goodman's treatment concerns the argument he offers against the reduction of metaphor to simile. Considering the idea that to say a picture is sad is to say elliptically it is like a sad person, Goodman remarks that the simile cannot be taken merely to assert that the picture is like the person in some way or other. Indeed, he says:[94]

> What the simile says in effect is that person and picture are alike in being sad, the one literally and the other metaphorically. . . . Whether the locution be 'is like' or 'is', the figure

likens picture to person by picking out a certain common
feature: that the predicate 'sad' applies to both, albeit to the
person initially and to the picture derivatively.

The problem with this argument, however, is that metaphor is a
sub-case of ambiguity: Thus while 'sad' may reasonably be
described as a single *label*, it can hardly be described as a single
predicate, for so to describe it would imply a single extension for
the label in question. Nor, *a fortiori*, can it be said that the likeness
ascribed by the simile under consideration consists in the sharing
of the common predicate 'sad', since there is no such common
predicate. It follows, finally, that the simile cannot be construed
after all as saying (univocally) that person and picture are alike in
being sad.

It might be suggested that the effect of this argument may be
achieved without appeal to the single predicate 'sad': the common
feature in question may be just that the label 'sad' (ambiguous
though it may be) applies to both person and picture. This
suggestion is itself difficult, however. For rather than merging
simile with metaphor, as intended by the original argument, it
would now merge simile rather with ambiguity in general.
Similes would, in effect, be authorized to liken objects if only
referred to by divergent replicas. The child camper would
properly be said to be like an elephant, since each is correctly
described by some replica of 'has a trunk'; the garment would be
considered like the stretch of coastline, each being rightly labeled
'a cape'. Similes would derive from etymological accidents
generally rather than from the closer relations associated with
metaphor, narrowly speaking. The line between simile, as envisaged in the original argument, and punning would become
blurred (puns would generate similes).

Nor is it possible to reconnect simile with metaphor by
requiring not just the applicability of a shared label, but the
applicability of such a label now literally, now metaphorically.
For such an explanation would assume the notion of metaphor to
be accounted for. On the other hand, to require rather the applicability of a shared label now initially, now derivatively, would be
independently inadequate. For accidentally ambiguous replicas
are also applied at different times, and may also be related by
strands of historical derivation. To separate out those strands

peculiar to metaphor without circular reliance on the notion of metaphor would, I suggest, be practically impossible.

The notion that the predicate 'sad', or even the mere label 'sad', indicates a common feature underlying the simile or metaphor in question seems thus untenable. The proposal we have been considering was that both figures be understood as likening picture to person by picking out such a common feature. As to what similarity, further, underlay this feature itself, i.e. characterized the objects of the predicate 'sad', Goodman replied, as we have seen, 'there is no real question.'[95] His strategy was thus twofold: (i) to interpret both the simile's explicit, and the metaphor's tacit, assertion of likeness as elliptical ('the simile cannot amount merely to saying that the picture is like the person in some respect or other; anything is like anything else to that extent'), acquiring determinacy through implicit reference to the ostensible sharing of the predicate 'sad', and then: (ii) to reject any further question as to a likeness presumed to form the basis for sharing this predicate. (i) must now, however, be surrendered because of its vulnerable assumption of a common predicate 'sad'.

It is important, furthermore, to take note of a further difficulty with (i), relating to its assumption that the simile acquires determinacy through reference to one of its *contained* predicates. This idea is implausible independently of the difficulty pointed out above. For similes typically acquire determinacy through reference to predicates they do not themselves contain, even when contained ones are (unlike 'sad') unambiguously applicable to the things said to be alike. To say, as educators have, that a child is like a young plant is to do much more than attribute youth to child as well as plant. It has been interpreted as conveying that there are further significant attributions to be made to both, for example, that child and plant are growing, that they require supervision, that they benefit from a controlled environment, that they pass through ordered developmental stages, etc. The simile may indeed be made determinate or 'filled in', but not in general through sole reference to contained predicates, even when unambiguously and appropriately applicable. Other predicates are brought in from without, in a manner that varies with context.

This point, interestingly enough, seems to be acknowledged in Goodman's own notion of 'plausible histories' explanatory of certain metaphorical applications, e.g. that 'warm colors are those of fire, cold colors those of ice.'[96] Here, despite (i), he does not say, with respect to warm colors and warm things, simply that they are alike in being warm, in the one case literally, in the other metaphorically. Rather, he imports the reference to an association with fire rather than ice as a further specification.

If (i) is to be dropped, is there an alternative strategy that will fulfill its basic motivation and preserve its contextualist features? It originated in the recognition that while metaphor may be taken as elliptical simile in that it omits the expression 'like', simile itself is further elliptical in omitting determining specifications for this expression. Without further specification, the bare likeness affirmed by simile is trivial; (i) seemed to offer a general way of supplying such specification through appeal to a contained predicate. Without such appeal, is it possible to suggest another way in which the indeterminacy of both figures may be overcome?

The answer is yes. The simile does not say that one thing is like another merely in some respect, nor does it, as we have argued, uniformly say they are alike in respect of contained predicates. But these are not the only alternatives. The simile may say, rather, that things are alike in respects that are salient or important in the context in question. Such an interpretation rests heavily on contextual, sometimes controversial, judgments of salience or importance; it is, at any rate, neither indeterminate nor trivial. Moreover, the process of specifying those respects thought to bear out the simile or metaphorical attribution is central to the practice of explication.

We have already illustrated, in the figure of the child and the plant, the manner in which predicates not contained in a given simile are imported so as to supply an interpretive basis for it. Clearly the same process holds for metaphor as well; whether we say the child is *like* a young plant or *is* a young plant makes no difference in this regard. Imported predicates are of course supplied in a way that depends upon an understanding of the context; there is no general (similarity, or other) formula for extracting them. Yet there may be limited principles helpful in the search for suitable predicates; acquired through experience or instruction, they may improve the interpretive abilities of readers.

Earlier, we criticized a version of the formulaic approach resting upon the principle of similarity supplemented by the proviso that the similarity be an important one; we pointed out that such a principle escapes vacuity only through heavy dependence on context. Such dependence is indeed a defect in a view that purports to offer a formula. It is, however, no defect in a view that rejects the very idea of a formula, insisting that metaphoric interpretation requires contextual judgment – not, indeed, of important similarities but of important predicates serving to define such similarities. (We have also noted the contextualism required to meet the problem of excessive narrowness affecting both intensionalism and interactionism.)

The version of contextualism here outlined yields, furthermore, an interpretation of the guidance afforded by literal applications to metaphoric ones. The earlier version, as we have seen, offered a view of metaphor resting on the notion of such guidance, but giving no explanation of it – indeed rejecting the question why predicates apply as they do metaphorically. The present contextualism, resting on an understanding of the context for the suggestion of significant predicates, clearly requires also a grasp of the literal application of the term in question. For the metaphorical application is to be understood as attaching to things sharing satisfaction of contextually important predicates with those picked out by the literal application.[97] Knowledge of the context alone is not sufficient; literal application must also be taken into account. Such application does not determine metaphorical extension, but it contributes to this determination. In other words, it guides the interpretation of metaphor, when properly supplemented by contextual understanding.

11 METAPHOR AND EXPLORATION

In creating a metaphor one may surprise oneself. Much of the discussion of metaphor has been conducted with reference to contexts of communication, and a mistaken, though tacit, assumption has been prevalent, i.e. that the producer of a metaphorical utterance has some special key to its comprehension which the hearer or reader can only struggle to find. In fact, the producer of any utterance, metaphorical or otherwise, may find it difficult or puzzling to interpret what has been said, and be surprised by the result of reflection on the matter. The interpretive role with respect to any utterance is not incompatible with that of producer, even when the purpose of the utterance has been straightforward communication.

But a special word needs to be said about the uses of metaphor in primarily investigative or theoretical spirit. Here what is often involved is the exploratory or heuristic function of comparison. The theorist frequently does not know in advance the basis of the comparison he puts forth. He supposes, or guesses, that a certain general crossing of categories may turn out to be significant.[98] The metaphor embodying this guess does not signify a prior determination by the theorist of the predicates importable from the investigative context in substantiation of his utterance. On the contrary, the utterance itself serves as an *invitation*, to himself and to others, to explore the context for significant shared predicates – new or old, simple or complex. The theorist offers not a declaration but a hypothesis: that there are important predicates in the relevant context for the 'filling in' or specification of the metaphor – that there are, in other words, significant theoretical connections to be forged between the categories involved. The challenge is not to read a substantiated message but to find or invent a significant description of nature.

The invitation presented by a metaphorical utterance may lead us to rethink old material in the light of new categorizations (the mind as an electronic computer) or to consider newly discovered phenomena in terms already available (black holes in space as vacuum cleaners). Whether the task be to incorporate the novel or to reorganize the familiar, metaphor serves often as a probe for connections that may improve understanding or spark theoretical advance.

The creative role of metaphorical utterance is again evident here. For it does not simply report isomorphisms but calls them forth afresh to direct, and be tried by, further investigations. The happy outcome of such investigations is of course not assured beforehand. While certain connections flourish, others languish and die. An advance in comprehension is always an achievement, never a foregone conclusion.

It might thus perhaps be suggested that the theorist – or the producer of metaphor, more generally – does not know what he is saying ('the meaning' of what he is saying). For the metaphorical term he uses has an extension he typically cannot elucidate at the time of utterance, dependent as such elucidation may be upon contextually significant predicates determined as such only in subsequent inquiry. The predicament is not, however, peculiar to metaphor, our literal attributions too gaining a theoretical refinement and determinacy through further investigation clearly not evident at the time of utterance. This situation is not likely to seem paradoxical unless we hold a firm division between meaning and fact. The process of finding out more about one's own meaning and finding out more about the world are, however, one and the same.

NOTES

1 Compare the discussion of the 'zero method' in Karl R. Popper, *The Poverty of Historicism*, London, Routledge & Kegan Paul, 1957, p. 141.
2 Consider in this connection the definition of ambiguity in William Empson, *Seven Types of Ambiguity*, third edition, London, Chatto & Windus, 1953, p. 1 and n. 1, *ibid.*; also Preface to the second edition, *ibid.*, pp. vii-xv, esp. p. viii. Compare also the introduction of the terms 'tenor' and 'vehicle' in I. A. Richards, *The Philosophy of Rhetoric*, New York, Oxford University Press, 1936, Lecture V. See, too, the comments on Empson's definition in Monroe C. Beardsley, *Aesthetics*, New York, Harcourt, Brace & World, Inc., 1958, p. 151, and on Richards's terminology, *op. cit.*, p. 159.
3 Compare, e.g. the discussion of ambiguous words in S. Freud, *Collected Papers*, Volume III, London, Hogarth Press, 1925, n. 1, p. 79; the discussion of syncretism of meaning in primitive imagery in Heinz Werner, *Comparative Psychology of Mental Development*, revised edition, Chicago, Follett Publishing Company, 1948, pp. 152 ff.; the treatment of metaphor in Ch. 6 of Ernst Cassirer, *Language and Myth*, New York, Harper & Brothers, 1946, and the discussion of aesthetic ambiguity by Ernst Kris and Abraham Kaplan in Ch. 10 of Ernst Kris, *Psychoanalytic Explorations in Art*, New York, International Universities Press, Inc., 1952, pp. 243-64.
4 See, in this connection W. V. Quine, *From a Logical Point of View*, second edition, revised, Cambridge, Massachusetts, Harvard University Press, 1961, p. 24.
5 Compare Katz's notion of a semantic theory as aiming to represent the speaker's knowledge of the language, manifested among other things by the *latter's* recognition of ambiguities. The semantic theorist's interpretations are to treat as ambiguous 'those sentences that the speaker regards as such . . .' See Jerrold J. Katz, 'Analyticity and Contradiction in Natural Language', in Jerry A. Fodor and Jerrold J. Katz, *The Struc-*

ture of Language: Readings in The Philosophy of Language, Englewood Cliffs, New Jersey, Prentice-Hall, Inc., 1964, pp. 519, 522.

6 See related comments in my *The Anatomy of Inquiry*, New York, Alfred A. Knopf, 1963; Indianapolis, Bobbs-Merrill, 1971, pp. 10-11.

7 W. V. Quine, *Methods of Logic*, New York, Henry Holt & Company, 1950, Sec. 8, 'Words into Symbols', esp. pp. 40, 44.

8 W. V. Quine, *Word and Object*, New York and London, published jointly by The Technology Press of The Massachusetts Institute of Technology and John Wiley & Sons, Inc., 1960, p. 129.

9 Ernst Kris and Abraham Kaplan, 'Aesthetic Ambiguity', in Kris, *Psychoanalytic Explorations in Art, op. cit.*

10 For sources and discussions of the development in question, see Quine, 'Two Dogmas of Empiricism' in his *From a Logical Point of View, op. cit.*; Nelson Goodman, *Problems and Projects*, Indianapolis and New York, Bobbs-Merrill, 1972, esp. Section V; and Morton White, *Toward Reunion in Philosophy*, Cambridge, Massachusetts, Harvard University Press, 1956, esp. Part II.

11 On this topic, cp. Bertrand Russell, *Introduction to Mathematical Philosophy*, London, George Allen & Unwin, 1919, 1920, Ch. XVII, esp. p. 183; W. V. Quine, *Mathematical Logic*, Cambridge, Massachusetts, Harvard University Press, 1947, p. 120; N. Goodman, *The Structure of Appearance*, third edition, Dordrecht, Reidel Publishing Company, 1977, Pt. One, Ch. II; and Goodman, *Problems and Projects, op. cit.*, Section IV.

12 A fundamental paper is Nelson Goodman and W. V. Quine, 'Steps Toward a Constructive Nominalism', *Journal of Symbolic Logic*, 1947, vol. 12, pp. 105-22, reprinted in Goodman's *Problems and Projects, op. cit.* For inscriptional analyses of language, see Ch. XI of Goodman's *The Structure of Appearance, op. cit.* The latter book, first published in 1951, contains also a nominalistic 'calculus of individuals' in Ch. II, developed by H. S. Leonard and Goodman and first presented in Leonard's Harvard doctoral thesis, *Singular Terms*, in 1930. Lesniewski had published such a calculus in 1916 and also in 1927-31 (see note 8, p. 33 of Goodman, *Structure of Appearance*, third edition, *op. cit.*). See also the recent study by R. Eberle, *Nominalistic Systems*, Dordrecht, Reidel Publishing Company, 1970. I have myself applied inscriptionalism to the analysis of indirect discourse and the theory of explanation; see my *The Anatomy of Inquiry, op. cit.*, Part I, Sections 6 and 8, and references therein.

I AMBIGUITY

1 The treatment to be presented in Part I appeared originally in my paper, 'Ambiguity: An Inscriptional Approach', in Richard Rudner and Israel Scheffler, editors, *Logic and Art: Essays in Honor of Nelson Goodman*, Indianapolis, The Bobbs-Merrill Company, Inc., 1972, pp. 251-72. Various minor modifications of that paper have been made in the present version, and the analysis of *M*-ambiguity in Section 5 is introduced here for the first time.

2 *The New Merriam-Webster Pocket Dictionary*, New York, Pocket Books, G. & C. Merriam, 1964, p. 72.

3 Nelson Goodman, *The Structure of Appearance*, third edition, Dordrecht, Reidel Publishing Company, 1977, p. 263.

4 See, on this topic, Chapter IV, 'The Use of "Exists"', in Morton White, *Toward Reunion in Philosophy*, Cambridge, Massachusetts, Harvard University Press, 1956, pp. 60-80.

5 John Hospers, *An Introduction to Philosophical Analysis*, New York, Prentice-Hall, 1953, p. 23. Cited in R. J. Richman, 'Ambiguity and Intuition', *Mind*, 68, 1959, p. 87.

6 Richman, *ibid.*, and see footnote, p. 87, where the point is credited to Bertram Jessup.

7 Willard Van Orman Quine, *Word and Object*, New York and London, published jointly by The Technology Press of the Massachusetts Institute of Technology and John Wiley & Sons, Inc., 1960, p. 132.

8 'Ambiguity and Intuition', *op. cit.*, p. 87.

9 The interpretation here proposed accords with the notion that ambiguity of occurrence presupposes 'semantical ambiguity'. It does not exhaust cases of what might ordinarily be considered ambiguous indecision. However, it characterizes a basic variety, in which the ambiguous token is tied to divergent extensions via the replica relation. Additional cases may be imagined where the token is tied to divergent non-replicas through e.g. syntactic or other relations (all such cases also describable inscriptionally). I am grateful to Robert Schwartz for bringing this sort of point to my attention.

10 'Ambiguity and Intuition', *op. cit.*, p. 87.

11 *Word and Object*, *op. cit.*, p. 129. His illustration of 'the ambiguity of a word [infecting] the containing sentence' is 'bore' in 'Our mothers bore us.'

12 *Ibid.*

13 W. V. Quine, *The Ways of Paradox*, New York, Random House, 1966, p. 194. *Cp. Word and Object*, *op. cit.*, p. 214.

14 The notion of a potential sentence was suggested to me by Nelson Goodman's discussion of possibles in his *Fact, Fiction and Forecast*, third edition, Indianapolis and New York, Bobbs-Merrill, 1973, p. 51. Treating the case in which a phenomenal place p and a phenomenal time t both exist although (because, say, one eye is closed at t) there is no place-time composed of p and t, Goodman considers the sum individual $p+t$ a possible place-time. 'This entity', he says, 'for lack of a certain relationship among its parts, misses being a place-time much as the scattered whole comprised of the body of one automobile and the chassis of another across the street misses being an automobile.' To call $p+t$ a possible place-time, he says, 'is not to speak of a new non-actual entity but to say something new about . . . the old actual entity $p+t$.'

15 R. J. Richman, 'Ambiguity and Intuition', *op. cit.*, p. 88.

16 Goodman, 'On Likeness of Meaning', *Analysis*, 1949, vol. 10, pp. 1-7; reprinted in his *Problems and Projects*, Indianapolis and New York, Bobbs-Merrill, 1972, pp. 221-30.

17 R. Rudner, 'A Note on Likeness of Meaning', *Analysis*, 1950, vol. 10, pp. 115-18.

18 B. L. Robbins, 'On Synonymy of Word-Events', *Analysis*, 1952, vol. 12, pp. 98-100.

19 Goodman, 'On Some Differences About Meaning', *Analysis*, 1953, vol. 13, pp. 90-96; reprinted in his *Problems and Projects, op. cit.*, pp. 231-8.

20 'On Likeness of Meaning', *Analysis, op. cit.*, p. 6; also *Problems and Projects, op. cit.*, pp. 228-9. In 'On Some Differences About Meaning', *op. cit.*, Goodman proposes other compounds to the same effect, e.g. 'literal English—word'.

21 'A Note on Likeness of Meaning', *op. cit.*, p. 116.

22 *Ibid.*, p. 117.

23 'On Synonymy of Word-Events', *op. cit.*

24 *Ibid.*, p. 99.

25 *Ibid.*, p. 100.

26 'On Some Differences About Meaning', *op. cit.*, p. 92.

27 The constituent extensions need to be primary only, for in the case of tokens with which we are here concerned, secondary extensions differentiate only among non-replicas, but if parallel constituents are non-replicas, the wholes will also be non-replicas, and thus already distinguished by the earlier reference to secondary extensions of the wholes. On the other hand, where the wholes are replicas, and also have the same primary extensions, they may be distinguished through the varying primary extensions of their parallel word-constituents.

28 Nelson Goodman, *Languages of Art*, [1968], second edition, Indianapolis, Indiana, Hackett Publishing Co. Inc., 1976, p. 205, fn. 16. Secondary extensions of constituents are here included, since the context concerns types rather than tokens. (See note 27 above.)

29 Robert Graves, *The Greek Myths*, New York, George Braziller, 1957, Vol. 2, p. 212, sec. 147.

30 See *The Greek Myths, ibid.*

31 'On Synonymy of Word-Events', *op. cit.*, p. 100.

32 In *Languages of Art, op. cit.*, Goodman stresses that labels or descriptions are themselves sorted by other labels, as well as effecting a sorting of elements themselves, the labeling of labels being independent of what these latter are labels for. 'Objects are classified under "desk". . . . Descriptions are classified under "desk-description" . . .' (p. 31). What I am here suggesting is that the labeling of labels may be effected not by a new compound but by a habit-guided transfer of the original label itself. (Reverse transfers, I suggest, may also occur.)

33 Since the E-ambiguous compounds K_1 and K_2 have not only 'Algernon' tokens but also 'description' tokens as constituents, why (it may be asked) is it that only A_1 (Raymond's 'Algernon' token) and coextensive A_2 (George's 'Algernon' token) are differentiated in meaning, and not also D_1 (Raymond's 'description' token) and coextensive D_2 (George's 'description' token)? The answer is that mention-selection does not relate tokens to all compounds in which they figure, but only to suitable mentions. Whereas A_1 does not denote but mention-selects the extension

of K_1, and A_2 does not denote but mention-selects rather the extension of K_2, D_1 mention-selects neither, but includes both in its own extension, and similarly for D_2: Everything denoted by either K_1 or K_2 is denoted by D_1, and also by D_2. An Algernon-description is a description but not an Algernon; it is (relative to A_1 or A_2, respectively) an Algernon-mention, but in no case a description-mention.

2   VAGUENESS

1 R. J. Richman, 'Ambiguity and Intuition', *Mind*, 1959, vol. 68, p. 87. (See notes 5 and 6 to Part I.)

2 Cp. the discussion in Max Black, 'Vagueness: An Exercise in Logical Analysis', *Philosophy of Science*, 1937, vol. 4, pp. 427-55; reprinted in M. Black, *Language and Philosophy*, Ithaca, New York, Cornell University Press, 1949, pp. 25-58, esp. p. 31, and footnote 12, which is critical of Russell on this point; see also Bertrand Russell, 'Vagueness', *Australasian Journal of Philosophy*, 1923, vol. I, 84-92.

3 See the related discussion, with respect to the differentiation of characters in a notation, of Nelson Goodman, *Languages of Art*, [1968], second edition, Indianapolis, Indiana, Hackett Publishing Company, Inc., 1976, p. 134.

4 See, for example, the discussion of word magic, and the notion of an 'essential identity between the word and what it denotes' in Ernst Cassirer, *Language and Myth*, New York, Dover Publications, Inc. [Copyright 1946 by Harper and Brothers], Ch. 4.

5 A similar argument applies to Davidson's view that learnability requires a certain logical structure, a view he employs in criticism of my theory of indirect discourse. For the latter theory see my 'An Inscriptional Approach to Indirect Quotation', *Analysis*, 1954, vol. XIV, pp. 83-90, and my *The Anatomy of Inquiry*, 1963, (Indianapolis, Bobbs-Merrill, 1971), Part I, Sections 6 and 8. For Davidson's view, see Donald Davidson, 'Theories of Meaning and Learnable Languages' in Y. Bar-Hillel, ed., *Logic, Methodology, and Philosophy of Science* [Proceedings of the 1964 International Congress], Amsterdam, North Holland, 1965, pp. 383-93. The that-clause predicates of my theory, though not "logically" analyzable, are structured and rule-governed; it is easy to see how the rule may guide learning. Cp. the similar point expressed in Quine's reply to Kaplan [*Synthese*, 19 (1968-69), p. 314]: 'Kaplan suggests twice that I have left what he calls intermediate contexts unanalyzed. I should stress that I have not meant to represent them as without logical or grammatical structure. This would be intolerable, for it would represent us, absurdly, as acquiring an infinite vocabulary. On the contrary, I attributed a logical grammar to the intermediate contexts. I construed "that" as an operator that attaches to a sentence to produce a name of a proposition.' Further discussion of the relevant structure of that-clause predicates may be found in Christopher S. Hill, 'Toward a Theory of Meaning for Belief Sentences', *Philosophical Studies*, October, 1976, vol. 30, No. 4, pp. 209-26, esp. p. 218 and footnote 10, p. 225. A general

critique of Davidson's assumptions on learnability is presented in R. J. Haack, 'Davidson on Learnable Languages', *Mind*, 1978, LXXXVII, pp. 230-49. For discussion of some of the points in this note, I am grateful to Professor Warren D. Goldfarb.

6 'Vagueness: An Exercise in Logical Analysis' in *Language and Philosophy, op. cit.*, pp. 28-9.

7 *Ibid.*, p. 34.

8 *Ibid.*, p. 33.

9 Friedrich Waismann, 'Verifiability', *Proceedings of the Aristotelian Society*, 1945, Supplementary Volume XIX, 119-50. Reprinted in A. Flew, ed., *Logic and Language*, First Series, Oxford, Basil Blackwell, 1951 and First and Second Series, Garden City, New York, Anchor Books, 1965, pp. 122-51. Page references to this article in the text are to the Anchor Books edition.

10 *Ibid.*, p. 125.

11 *Ibid.*

12 See Part I, Section 7, and Part II, Section 4.

13 Rudolf Carnap, 'Meaning and Synonymy in Natural Languages', *Philosophical Studies*, 1955, vol. 6, 33-47. Reprinted as Article D in the Supplement of R. Carnap, *Meaning and Necessity*, enlarged edition, Chicago, The University of Chicago Press, 1956, pp. 233-47. References in the text will be to the latter source.

14 *Ibid.*, p. 238.

15 *Ibid.*

16 *Ibid.*, pp. 239-40.

17 *Ibid.*, pp. 241-2.

18 Waismann, *op. cit.*, p. 126.

19 Alonzo Church, Entry 'Relative', in D. D. Runes, *The Dictionary of Philosophy*, New York, Philosophical Library, 1942, p. 269.

20 Carl G. Hempel, *Fundamentals of Concept Formation in Empirical Science*, Chicago, University of Chicago Press, 1952, pp. 55-6.

21 Alonzo Church, Entry 'Vague', in D. D. Runes, *op. cit.*, p. 329.

22 Carl G. Hempel, *op. cit.*, p. 56.

23 See Part II, Section 2.

24 The discussion to follow centers on Black's pioneering and influential paper of 1937, *op. cit.*, which still retains its philosophical interest. Black has since written much on language, and his paper 'Reasoning with Loose Concepts' in his *Margins of Precision*, Ithaca, New York, Cornell University Press, 1970, pp. 1-13, is of especial relevance to the topic of vagueness. In the latter paper, taking a position that contrasts with that of the former, he writes of the attempt to modify 'traditional logic' that it 'makes the mistake of confusing the unstated conditions for the application of a rule of logic with a supposed deficiency in the rule itself . . . . borderline cases do not constitute *exceptions* to the rule of excluded middle; they are simply *irrelevant* to it.' (pp. 10-11). The 1937 paper is philosophically interesting because it argues for a semantic notion of vagueness rather than simply assuming it, as many more recent papers do. (Cp. K. Fine, 'Vagueness, Truth and Logic', *Synthese*,

1975, vol. 30, p. 265: 'Let us say, in a preliminary way, what vagueness is. I take it to be a semantic notion. Very roughly, vagueness is deficiency of meaning.') Many related papers of technical interest have also been published in recent years, e.g. by L. A. Zadeh, and several others; these papers may well have the valuable applications to studies of pattern recognition, communication, information retrieval etc., claimed for them. From a philosophical point of view, however, they provide insufficient emphasis on logical foundations, and typically they seem simply to assume the semantic notion of 'fuzziness of meaning'. Cp. L. A. Zadeh, 'Quantitative Fuzzy Semantics', *Information Sciences*, 1971, vol. 3, pp. 159-76, esp. p. 160.

25 Black, 'Vagueness: An Exercise in Logical Analysis', in *Language and Philosophy, op. cit.*, pp. 33-5.

26 *Ibid.*, pp. 35-6.

27 *Ibid.*, p. 55.

28 *Ibid.*, p. 43.

29 *Ibid.*, p. 48.

30 Carl G. Hempel, 'Vagueness and Logic', *Philosophy of Science*, 1939, vol. 6, pp. 163-80, esp. pp. 178-9.

31 *Ibid.*, p. 178.

32 Black, *Language and Philosophy, op. cit.*, p. 250.

33 W. V. Quine, *Philosophy of Logic*, Englewood Cliffs, N.J., Prentice-Hall, Inc., 1970, p. 85.

34 *Ibid.*

35 C. S. Peirce, Entry 'Vague', in J. M. Baldwin, ed., *Dictionary of Philosophy and Psychology*, New York, Macmillan [vol. II], 1902, p. 748.

36 *Op. cit.*, p. 28.

37 Max Black, Entry 'Vagueness', in D. D. Runes, *op. cit.*, p. 329.

38 Susan Haack, *Deviant Logic*, London, Cambridge University Press, 1974, p. 111, italics in the original.

39 *Ibid.*, p. 110.

40 William P. Alston, *Philosophy of Language*, Englewood Cliffs, N.J., Prentice-Hall, Inc., 1964, pp. 84-5.

41 *Ibid.*, p. 85.

42 W. V. Quine, 'On Carnap's Views on Ontology', *Philosophical Studies*, 1951, vol. 2; reprinted in W. V. Quine, *The Ways of Paradox*, New York, Random House, 1966, p. 134.

43 *Word and Object, op. cit.*, pp. 125-6.

44 Quine, *Philosophy of Logic, op. cit.*, p. 85.

3 METAPHOR

1 See Part I, section 3.

2 See Part I, section 10.

3 The classification is greatly indebted to Beardsley's treatment in his *Aesthetics*, New York, Harcourt, Brace & World, Inc., 1958, pp. 134-47. My characterization of the first four approaches reflects Beardsley's

discussion of 'the Supervenience theory', 'the Emotive theory', 'the Literalist theory' and 'the Controversion theory', although it will soon become evident that I have changed not only certain names but also certain substantive emphases and contrasts, in order to facilitate my subsequent analyses. I of course make no exclusivist claims for my classificatory constructions, and it is worth noting that Beardsley has offered variant accounts elsewhere; see, e.g. the discussion of theories of metaphor in his article, 'Metaphor', in Paul Edwards, editor, *The Encyclopedia of Philosophy*, New York and London, Collier Macmillan Publishers, 1967, Volume 5, pp. 285-6. (See also the discussion of theories of metaphor in Part II, ch. IV of Warren A. Shibles, *An Analysis of Metaphor in the Light of W. M. Urban's Theories*, The Hague, Mouton, 1971, pp. 63-74, and the references therein; as well as the same author's *Metaphor: An Annotated Bibliography and History* (Whitewater, Wisconsin, The Language Press, 1971).

4 Monroe C. Beardsley, *Aesthetics, op. cit.*, p. 135.

5 *Ibid.*, p. 136.

6 *Ibid.*

7 *Ibid.*

8 *Ibid.*, p. 160. The cited passage is from Martin Foss, *Symbol and Metaphor in Human Experience*, Princeton, New Jersey, Princeton University Press, 1949, p. 61.

9 Foss, *op. cit.*, pp. 61-2.

10 Beardsley, *op. cit.*, p. 135.

11 *Ibid.*, p. 160.

12 I suggest the distinction of these variants not to report historical views but to bring out points of analytical importance. Beardsley discusses 'the Emotive theory' in *Aesthetics, op. cit.*, pp. 134-5, and in 'Metaphor', in *The Encyclopedia of Philosophy, op. cit.*, p. 285.

Note that my characterization of the emotive approach in terms of *evincing or arousing* feelings separates it sharply from accounts in terms of *reference* to feelings, with which it may sometimes be confused. In connection with the Emotive theory Beardsley cites (both in *Aesthetics* and in his *Encyclopedia* article) Max Rieser, 'Brief Introduction to an Epistemology of Art', *Journal of Philosophy*, 1950, vol. XLVII, pp. 695-704, and Rieser does indeed say, in this article, 'The poetic comparison is neither a statement of fact nor a logical statement, nor is it a linguistic transaction in the usual sense. It is not a proposition.' (p. 701). However, in *Aesthetics* Beardsley also cites Rieser's earlier article, 'Analysis of the Poetic Simile', *Journal of Philosophy*, 1940, vol. XXXVII, 209-17 (though referring here to Rieser as holding 'a semi-emotive Theory'). But in the latter paper, Rieser treats metaphor and simile as comparisons of the impressions left by 'real objects' in the sensibility (p. 210), 'associating things of similar emotional value' (p. 216). To associate things of similar emotional value is of course quite a different matter from evincing or arousing emotion; the view in question thus does *not* exemplify what I call 'the emotive approach'.

13 *Aesthetics, op. cit.*, p. 135.

14 See, for example, Magda B. Arnold, *Emotion and Personality*, [vol. I: Psychological Aspects], New York, Columbia University Press, 1960, pp. 259-63.

15 *Aesthetics, op. cit.*, p. 135.

16 On this theme, see my 'In Praise of the Cognitive Emotions', *Teachers College Record*, 1977, vol. 79, No. 2, December, pp. 171-86, and references therein.

17 For a review of the case of ethics see Richard B. Brandt, 'Emotive Theory of Ethics', in Paul Edwards, *Encyclopedia of Philosophy, op. cit.*, volume 2, pp. 493-6. (See also the remarks on 'the argument from emotiveness', pp. 465-6 in my 'Anti-Naturalist Restrictions in Ethics', *Journal of Philosophy*, 1953, vol. L, pp. 457-66.)

18 Richard Whately, *Elements of Rhetoric*, 7th revised edition, London, John W. Parker, 1846, p. 280; quoted in M. Black, *Models and Metaphors*, Ithaca, New York, Cornell University Press, 1962, pp. 35-6.

19 William P. Alston, *Philosophy of Language*, Englewood Cliffs, N.J., Prentice-Hall, Inc., 1964, p. 97.

20 *Ibid.*, p. 98.

21 *Ibid.*

22 P. Henle, ed., *Language, Thought, and Culture*, Ann Arbor, Michigan, University of Michigan Press, 1958, p. 178; quoted in Alston, *op. cit.*

23 Alston, *op. cit.*, p. 99.

24 *Ibid.*

25 *Ibid.*

26 Henle, *op. cit.*, p. 178; Alston *op. cit.*, p. 98.

27 Beardsley, *Aesthetics, op. cit.*, p. 125. ('Intensionalism' is not Beardsley's name for his view; it is one I adopt to emphasize the central role of connoted properties in his account.)

28 *Ibid.*, p. 141.

29 *Ibid.*, p. 142.

30 *Ibid.*, p. 143, italics in the original.

31 *Ibid.*, p. 144.

32 *Ibid.*

33 *Ibid.*

34 *Ibid.*, p. 140.

35 *Ibid.*, p. 145.

36 *Ibid.*, p. 144.

37 On this point, see Timothy Binkley, 'On the Truth and Probity of Metaphor', *Journal of Aesthetics and Art Criticism*, 1974, vol. 33, pp. 171-80; Ted Cohen, 'Notes on Metaphor', *ibid.*, 1976, vol. 34, pp. 249-59; the reply to these papers by Monroe C. Beardsley, 'Metaphor and Falsity', *ibid.*, 1976, vol. 35, pp. 218-22; and Max Black, 'More about Metaphor', *Dialectica*, 1977, vol. 31, Fasc. 3-4, pp. 431-57, esp. p. 450.

38 See Part I, section 5 above. My discussion of *M*-ambiguity there was illustrated by the *pun*, where established but conflicting extensional interpretations are to be accommodated by the same inscription. The *M*-ambiguous metaphorical token, by contrast, establishes a *new* extension, while retaining an older, literal one. For puns, I suggested the *M*-

ambiguous token be taken as non-denoting but correlated with divergent replicas; the novel extension of a metaphorical token will, however, typically have no other (prior) replica as its vehicle. Thus, I propose that an *M*-ambiguous metaphorical token be itself assigned the novel extension in question, while the older, literal extension is borne by a replica. It should of course be emphasized that not all metaphorical tokens are *M*-ambiguous; most are not.

39 I emphasize 'internal' criticism here and merely note, in passing, that the postulation of properties and meanings is, if ultimate, of course unacceptable to inscriptionalism. The notion of a term's designated characteristics as those that are peculiarly *defining* seems, moreover, to require a strong view of definition for which no basis is offered.

40 *Aesthetics, op. cit.*, p. 142.

41 *Ibid.*

42 *Ibid.*, pp. 140-1.

43 *Ibid.*, p. 143.

44 *Ibid.*, pp. 140-1.

45 *Ibid.*, p. 144.

46 *Ibid.*, p. 143.

47 *Ibid.*, p. 125.

48 *Ibid.*, p. 143.

49 *Ibid.*, p. 139.

50 *Ibid.*, p. 125. I thank Jacob Adler for a remark that led to improvement of one of my examples in the following paragraph.

51 *Ibid.*, p. 145.

52 I have taken Beardsley's account in *Aesthetics* as exemplifying intensionalism throughout, and my criticism of his notion of 'connotation' refers in particular to the treatment set forth in *Aesthetics*. In the later 'The Metaphorical Twist', *Philosophy and Phenomenological Research*, 1962, vol. XXII, pp. 293-307, he offers a variant account which seems to me however still vulnerable to the critical comments I have offered. He there writes (p. 300), 'The connotations of a word standing for objects of a certain kind, it will be agreed, are drawn from the total set of accidental properties either found in or attributed to such objects.' But in a more recent paper, 'Metaphorical Senses', *Noûs*, 1978, vol. 12, pp. 3-16, he offers a revised version of his theory which replaces the notion of 'connotation' with that of 'credence-property', such a property being one 'commonly believed to belong to most or to normal members of the [relevant] extension'. Indeed he credits 'Max Black's pioneering essay on metaphor' with helping to promote a consensus on the point that (p. 8) 'the properties that count in metaphor are not the actual properties of things denoted by the metaphorical term, but believed properties'. This revision in Beardsley's view does mark a basic change from the account offered in *Aesthetics*, and escapes the force of the criticism I have so far offered of intensionalism on the score of excessive breadth. It remains however, subject to certain critical comments I shall address to Black's interactionism, with which (as respects the notion of metaphorically relevant property) it is associated by Beardsley himself.

53 I. A. Richards, *The Philosophy of Rhetoric*, New York, Oxford University Press, 1936, p. 93; quoted in Max Black, *Models and Metaphors*, Ithaca, New York, Cornell University Press, 1962, p. 38. Black's essay, 'Metaphor', which appears as Chapter III of the book, was originally published in *Proceedings of the Aristotelian Society*, 1954, vol. 55, (new series), London, Harrison, 1955, pp. 273-94.

54 *Models and Metaphors, op. cit.*, p. 39.

55 Richards, *op. cit.*, p. 119; quoted in Black, *op. cit.*, p. 38, fn. 18.

56 Black, *ibid.*, pp. 39-40.

57 *Ibid.*, p. 40.

58 *Ibid.*, p. 41.

59 *Ibid.*, italics in the original.

60 *Ibid.*

61 *Ibid.*, pp. 44-5.

62 *Ibid.*, pp. 43-4.

63 *Ibid.*, p. 41.

64 *Ibid.*, pp. 42-3.

65 *Ibid.*, p. 43.

66 *Ibid.*, p. 39.

67 *Ibid.*

68 *Ibid.*, p. 46.

69 *Ibid.*, p. 44.

70 *Ibid.*, pp. 40-1.

71 *Ibid.*, p. 41, italics in the original.

72 *Ibid.*, p. 41, italics in the original. I thank Daniel Brudney for suggesting an improvement in one of my examples in the previous paragraph.

73 *Ibid.*, p. 40.

74 *Ibid.*, p. 40.

75 *Ibid.*, p. 44.

76 *Ibid.*, p. 43.

77 Nelson Goodman, *Languages of Art* (1968), second edition, Indianapolis, Indiana, Hackett Publishing Co., Inc., 1976, p. 69. (Goodman does not himself describe his treatment as contextual: contextualism is an interpretation that I suggest fits his treatment.)

78 *Ibid.* As T. Cohen has pointed out, the formulation given here conflicts both with other passages in *Languages of Art* and with plausible examples. (See Cohen, *op. cit.*, *Journal of Aesthetics and Art Criticism*, 1976, vol. 34, pp. 258-9.) Goodman's main point is, however, not that the literal reading of a sentence is false if its metaphorical reading is true, but rather that the latter reading of a label involves an extensional shift. In other words, metaphorical application of a label to an object defies a prior denial of that label to some object satisfying the same application (or a prior denotation of some object denied the same application).

I have myself already argued (Part III, Section 6) that the literal interpretation of an expression may be retained along with a metaphorical interpretation, as an instance of *M*-ambiguity. However, on my *analysis* of such a situation, the single token of course does not carry differing extensions. See Part I, Section 5, and Part III, note 38.

79 *Ibid.*, pp. 69-70.
80 *Ibid.*, p. 70.
81 *Ibid.*, pp. 70-1.
82 *Ibid.*, pp. 71-2.
83 *Ibid.*, p. 72.
84 *Ibid.*, p. 74.
85 *Ibid.*
86 *Ibid.*, pp. 74-5.
87 E. H. Gombrich, *Art and Illusion*, New York, Pantheon Books, 1960, p. 370.
88 *Languages of Art, op. cit.*, p. 75.
89 *Ibid.*, p. 76.
90 *Ibid.*, pp. 76-7.
91 *Ibid.*, pp. 77-8, italics in the original.
92 *Ibid.*, p. 78.
93 *Ibid.*, p. 81 ff.
94 *Ibid.*, pp. 77-8, italics in the original.
95 *Ibid.*, p. 78.
96 *Ibid.*, p. 76.
97 Null terms (in literal application) require slightly different treatment, lacking things to satisfy them. The metaphorical application of 'dragon' to persons can hardly be said literally to liken persons to dragons, there being no dragons. Goodman, in his *Ways of Worldmaking* (Indianapolis, Cambridge: Hackett Publishing Company, 1978), p. 104, fn. 10, points out that 'since "Don Quixote" and "Don Juan" have the same (null) literal extension, their metaphorical sorting of people cannot reflect any literal sorting.' He traces their metaphorical sorting to (literal) extensional divergence between parallel compounds of the terms, or differences in what these terms themselves satisfy and exemplify. 'In sum, "Don Quixote" and "Don Juan" are denoted by different terms (e.g. "Don-Quixote-term" and "Don-Juan-term") that also denote other different terms (e.g. "zany jouster" and "inveterate seducer") that in turn denote different people.'

Put in terms of mention-selection, the term with null literal extension mention-selects various descriptions of which some, important in context, may also characterize persons to whom metaphorical reference is made. A person metaphorically described as Don Quixote is not literally likened to Don Quixote nor does he share the satisfaction of important predicates with the literal Don Quixote; rather he satisfies certain important predicates constituting Don-Quixote-descriptions. Where a null term is rather the grammatical subject of a metaphorical attribution with a non-null predicate, e.g. in 'Don Quixote was a mule', some contextually important descriptions mention-selected by 'Don Quixote' are thought applicable to mules. And where, as in the metaphorical 'Cinderella was an angel', both subject and predicate are (literally) null, some contextually relevant description mention-selected by 'Cinderella' is also mention-selected by 'angel'. For reference to the latter sort of case see the final paragraphs of the interesting paper by Nelson Goodman,

'Stories upon Stories; or Reality in Tiers', delivered at the conference, *Levels of Reality*, in Florence, Italy in September 1978.

98 For a discussion of metaphorical 'sort-crossing' in the context of theories of nature, see Colin Murray Turbayne, *The Myth of Metaphor* [1962], Revised edition, Columbia, South Carolina, University of South Carolina Press, 1970. See also the Appendix by Rolf Eberle, 'Models, Metaphors, and Formal Interpretations', *ibid.*, pp. 219-33, esp. Section 6, 'Models as Tools of Discovery'.

INDEX

accidental pairs, 80–1, 87
Adler, Jacob, 140 n50
Alston, W. P., 74–5, 93–6, 137 n40,
  n41, 139 n19–n26
ambiguity, 11–36, 37–8
  genetic interpretations of, 3, 131 n3
  and metaphor, 14, 34–5, 79–82, 119,
    125
  semantical versus psychological, 16,
    38, 133 n9
  and synonymy, 21–7
  theoretical accounts and their
    difficulties, 7–8
  understanding of, 2–8
  and vagueness, 14–16
  see also C-ambiguity, E-ambiguity,
    I-ambiguity, K-ambiguity,
    M-ambiguity
analyticity, 7–9, 53–7, 73, 76
Arnold, Magda B., 139 n14

Baldwin, J. M., 137 n35, n36
Beardsley, Monroe C., 82, 89, 91,
  97–107, 131 n2, 137–8 n3–n8,
  138 n10–n13, 139 n15, n27–n37,
  140 n40–n52
Binkley, Timothy, 139 n37
Black, Max, 49–50, 65–71, 73, 107–18,
  135 n2, 136 n6–n8, n24, 137
  n25–n29, n32, n37, 139 n18, n37,
  140 n52, 141 n53–n76
Brandt, Richard, 139 n17
Brudney, Daniel, 141 n72

C-Ambiguity, 27–9, 32

and CM-ambiguity, 29
and CI-ambiguity, 29
Carnap, R., 54–6, 76, 136 n13–n17
Cassirer, Ernst, 131 n2, 135 n4
Church, A., 58–9, 61–2, 136 n19, n21
Cohen, Ted, 139 n37, 141 n78
commonplaces:
  system of associated, 108–18
compounds, 23, 25–36, 43–9, 51–3,
    56–7, 134 n20, n32, 134–5 n33,
    142 n97
  atomic, 45–9
  parallel, 22–3, 25, 28, 33, 34
  molecular, 43–5
Congruence:
  Principle of, 99, 101, 103–5, 107
connotation:
  see metaphor, and connoted
    properties of words
contextualism, 82, 100, 118–28, 141 n77
controversion theory of metaphor, 98,
    137–8 n3, 139 n27; see also
    intensionalism

Davidson, Donald, 135–6 n5
dictionary, 3–4, 8, 11–12, 18, 81–3, 87,
  92, 108

E-ambiguity, 12–17, 20–1, 23, 26–32,
  35–8, 79–82, 134 n33
Eberle, R., 132 n12, 143 n98
Edwards, Paul, 138 n3, 139 n17
emotivism, 82, 87–92, 97, 100, 107,
  118, 137–8 n3, 138 n12
emotivity, 83–4, 88–92, 138 n12

Empson, William, 131 n2
extension:
  primary, 22–8, 30–1, 35–6, 134 n27
  secondary, 22–8, 30–1, 36, 134 n27

Fine, K., 136–7 n24
Flew, A., 136 n9–n11
Fodor, Jerry A., 131 n5
formulaic approach to metaphor, 82,
  92–6, 99–100, 107, 118, 127–8,
  137–8 n3
Foss, M., 83, 138 n8–n9
Freud, S., 131 n2

generality, 12, 14–15, 37, 40–3
Goldfarb, Warren, 135–6 n5
Gombrich, E. H., 121, 142 n87
Goodman, Nelson, 4, 22–8, 119–27,
  132 n10–n12, 132 n1, 133 n3,
  133 n14, 133 n16, 134 n19–n20,
  134 n22, 134 n26, 134 n28,
  134 n32, 135 n3, 141 n77–n78,
  142 n79–n86, 142 n88–n97
Graves, Robert, 134 n29–n30

Haack, R. J., 135–6 n5
Haack, S., 74, 137 n38–n39
Hempel, C. G., 58–9, 61–3, 70–1,
  136 n20, 136 n22, 137 n30, n31
Henle, P., 94, 96, 139 n22, 139 n26
Hill, Christopher S., 135–6 n5
Hospers, John, 16, 133 n5

I-ambiguity, 15–18, 21, 29, 37–40
  and CI-ambiguity, 29
ideal conception of language, 1–2, 4–7,
  11
idioms, 83, 87
indicator words, 14, 15, 38, 80–2, 87,
  95
inscriptionalism, 8–9, 11, 13, 14, 16, 18,
  22, 23, 132 n12, n1, 140 n39
intensional entities, 7–9, 11–13, 20, 23,
  55–6
intensionalism, 82, 97–107, 110, 113–14,
  117–18, 128, 137–8 n3, 139 n27,
  140 n52
interactionism, 82, 107–18, 128, 140
  n52
intuitionism, 82–7, 92, 95, 99–100,
  107, 118, 137–8 n3

Jessup, Bertram, 133 n6

K-ambiguity, 29–32, 35–6
Kaplan, Abraham, 131 n2, 132 n9
Kaplan, David, 135 n5
Katz, Jerrold J., 131 n5
Kris, Ernst, 131 n2, 132 n9

Leonard, H. S., 132 n12
Lesniewski, S., 132 n12
logic:
  and vagueness, 65–78

M-ambiguity, 17–21, 101, 139–40 n38,
  141 n78
  and CM-ambiguity, 29
meaning, 7–9, 11–12, 16, 23, 72–8, 83,
  85, 88–90, 101, 104, 106, 108,
  129–30, 140 n39
  likeness and difference of, see
  synonymy
  metaphorical change in, 109–13, 115
mention-selection, 31–6, 45–9, 51–3,
  55–7, 79–82, 134 n32, 134–5 n33,
  142 n97
metaphor, 79–130
  and ambiguity, 14, 34–5, 79–82,
  119, 125
  and anti-replaceability thesis, 84–8,
  90, 92
  and anti-formula thesis, 85–8, 92–6
  broad versus narrow interpretation,
  124
  and connoted properties of words,
  97–107, 113–17, 139 n27, 140 n52
  contextual approach, 82, 100, 118–28,
  141 n77
  and E-ambiguity, 79–82
  emotive approach, 82, 87–92, 97,
  100, 107, 118, 137–8 n3, 138 n12
  and exploration, 128–30
  formulaic approach, 82, 92–6, 99–100,
  107, 118, 127–8, 137–8 n3
  genetic interpretations of, 3, 131 n3
  and iconicity, 92, 94, 96
  intensional approach, 82, 97–107,
  110, 113–14, 117–18, 128,
  137–8 n3, 139 n27, 140 n52
  interactional approach, 82, 107–18,
  128, 140 n52
  and interpretive ingenuity, 81–2, 87,
  92–3, 99–100, 118, 128–30
  intuitionistic approach, 82–7, 92, 95,
  99–100, 107, 118, 137–8 n3

and mention-selection, 34–5, 46, 48, 56, 79–82
principal versus subsidiary subject of, 108–9, 112–15, 117
and similarity, 87, 92–6, 99, 107, 118, 123, 125–8
and translatability, 84, 112–13
see also metaphoric transfer; schema; simile; realm
metaphoric transfer, 35, 46, 48, 56, 79, 109–13, 115, 122–3
metonymy, 93
multiple meaning, 6; *see also* M-ambiguity
myths, 30, 134 n29–n30

natural language, 1–2, 6, 7, 28
nonsense, 103–4, 121

open texture, 50–65

Peirce, C. S., 73, 94, 137 n35, n36
Plenitude:
Principle of, 99, 102–5
poetry, 6–7, 18, 99, 117, 138 n12
Popper, Karl R., 131 n1
potential sentence, 19–20, 133 n14
precision, 40–3, 60–5
puns, 18, 20, 125, 139–40 n38

Quine, W. V., 5–6, 16–18, 71–2, 76–7, 131 n2, n4, 132 n7–n8, n10–n12, 133 n7, n11–n13, 135 n5, 137 n33–n34, n42–n44

realm, 120
replica:
defined, 13
Richards, I. A., 107–8, 112, 131 n2, 141 n53, n55
Richman, R. J., 16–17, 21, 38, 133 n5, n6, n8, n10, n15, 135 n1
Rieser, Max, 138 n12
Robbins, B. L., 22, 24–8, 30–2, 134 n18, n23–n25, n31
Rudner, Richard, 22, 24, 26–7, 132 n1, 134 n17, n21, n22

Runes, D. D., 136 n19, n21, 137 n37
Russell, Bertrand, 71, 132 n11, 135 n2

Shakespeare, W., 94
Scheffler, Israel, 131 n6, 132 n12, n1, 135 n5, 139 n16, n17
schema, 120–1, 124
Schwartz, Robert, 133 n9
sense, 11–12, 20, 93–4
Shibles, Warren A., 138 n3
simile, 93–4, 96, 107, 123–7, 138 n12
supervenience theory of metaphor, 82, 137–8 n3
see also intuitionism
synecdoche, 92, 93
synonymy, 7–9, 11–13, 21ff., 84

Turbayne, C. M., 143 n98

vagueness, 37–78
and classification, 58–65
and compounds, 43–9
contrasted with E-ambiguity, 15, 37–8
and I-ambiguity, 37–40
and generality, 37, 40–3
and logic, 65–78
related to meaning and fact, 72–8
and mention-selection, 45–9, 51–3, 55–6
pragmatic versus semantic interpretation, 43, 65–72, 77–8, 136–7 n24
and precision, 40–3, 60–5
and relative terms, 57–60, 62
relativity and universality of, 49–51
see also open texture

Waismann, Friedrich, 51, 56, 136 n9–n11, n18
Werner, Heinz, 131 n2
Whately, Richard, 93, 139 n18
White, Morton, 132 n10, 133 n4

Zadeh, L. A., 137 n24

International Library of Philosophy & Scientific Method

Editor: Ted Honderich

(*Demy 8vo*)

Allen, R. E. (Ed.), **Studies in Plato's Metaphysics** *464 pp. 1965*.
Plato's 'Euthyphro' and the Earlier Theory of Forms *184 pp. 1970*.
Allen, R. E. and Furley, David J. (Eds.), **Studies in Presocratic Philosophy**
Volume II *448 pp. 1975*.
Armstrong, D. M., **Perception and the Physical World** *208 pp. 1961*.
A Materialist Theory of the Mind *376 pp. 1967*.
Bambrough, Renford (Ed.), **New Essays on Plato and Aristotle**
184 pp. 1965.
Barry, Brian, **Political Argument** *382 pp. 1965*.
Bird, Graham, **Kant's Theory of Knowledge** *220 pp. 1962*.
Bogen, James, **Wittgenstein's Philosophy of Language** *256 pp. 1972*.
Broad, C. D., **Lectures on Psychical Research** *461 pp. 1962*.
(*2nd Impression 1966.*)
Crombie, I. M., **An Examination of Plato's Doctrine**
I. Plato on Man and Society *408 pp. 1962*.
II. Plato on Knowledge and Reality *583 pp. 1963*.
Day, John Patrick, **Inductive Probability** *352 pp. 1961*.
Dennett, D. C., **Content and Consciousness** *202 pp. 1969*.
Dretske, Fred I., **Seeing and Knowing** *270 pp. 1969*.
Ducasse, C. J., **Truth, Knowledge and Causation** *263 pp. 1969*.
Edel, Abraham, **Method in Ethical Theory** *379 pp. 1963*.
Farm, K. T. (Ed.), **Symposium on J. L. Austin** *512 pp. 1969*.
Findlay, J. N., **Plato: The Written and Unwritten Doctrines** *498 pp. 1974*.
Flew, Anthony, **Hume's Philosophy of Belief** *296 pp. 1961*.
Fogelin, Robert J., **Evidence and Meaning** *200 pp. 1967*.
Franklin, R., **Freewill and Determinism** *353 pp. 1968*.
Furley, David J. and Allen, R. E. (Eds.), **Studies in Presocratic Philosophy**
Volume I *326 pp. 1970*.
Gale, Richard, **The Language of Time** *256 pp. 1967*.
Glover, Jonathan, **Responsibility** *212 pp. 1970*.
Goldman, Lucien, **The Hidden God** *424 pp. 1964*.
Hamlyn, D. W., **Sensation and Perception** *222 pp. 1961*.
(*3rd Impression 1967.*)
Husserl, Edmund, **Logical Investigations** *Vol. I: 456 pp. Vol. II: 464 pp.*
Kemp, J., **Reason, Action and Morality** *216 pp. 1964*.
Körner, Stephan, **Experience and Theory** *272 pp. 1966*.
Lazerowitz, Morris, **Studies in Metaphilosophy** *276 pp. 1964*.
Linsky, Leonard, **Referring** *152 pp. 1967*.
Mackenzie, Brian D., **The Origins of Behaviourism,** *1976.*
MacIntosh, J. J. and Coval, S. C. (Eds.), **Business of Reason** *280 pp. 1969*.
Meiland, Jack W., **Talking About Particulars** *192 pp. 1970*.
Merleau-Ponty, M., **Phenomenology of Perception** *487 pp. 1962*.
Naess, Arne, **Scepticism** *176 pp. 1969*.
Perelman, Chaim, **The Idea of Justice and the Problem of Argument**
224 pp. 1963.
Rorty, A. (Ed.), **Personal Identity** *1975*.